Ghosts of Surrey

Ghosts
of
Surrey

John Janaway

COUNTRYSIDE BOOKS
NEWBURY, BERKSHIRE

First Published 1991
© John Janaway 1991

Countryside Books
3 Catherine Road, Newbury, Berkshire

ISBN 1 85306 144 1

Produced through MRM Associates Ltd., Reading
Typeset by Wessex Press Design & Print Ltd., Warminster
Printed by J. W. Arrowsmith Ltd., Bristol

To G.S.

Acknowledgements

My very grateful thanks to Mavis Davies, Sally Jenkinson, Anne Johns, 'Mac' McLellan, Tom Maile, Duncan Mirylees, Peter Phillips, 'Robin', Peter Sagar, Ron Shettle and Sylvia Walker; also to my ever patient family — Sue, Stephen and Christopher, and to 'A.E.', who taught me not to disbelieve.

Contents

Introduction

I SUSPECT that very few of us have not been asked at some time or other if we believe in ghosts. The answer will invariably be either 'no' or 'I can't say one way or the other until I have seen one'. But some will agree, often with some hesitation, that they do indeed believe that spirits from the past and, perhaps, the present and even the future, do move among us unseen or unfelt by most.

Many of those people who do believe in ghosts will have experienced at some moment in their lives an incident for which they can find no explanation within the normal dimensions of their consciousness. Often they will be reluctant to elaborate for fear of being ridiculed but sometimes, in a quiet moment of relaxation, they may tell their story.

But what did they see, feel or hear? What is it that they believe in? What, in fact, is a ghost? For the answer I instinctively reached for my dictionary for a definition — 'ghost — soul of dead person in Hades etc.; spectre esp. of dead person appearing to the living'. Good as far as it goes, I think, but I suspect that the 'etc' and the 'esp.' hide numerous other types of 'ghostly' experience.

Spectres or apparitions are the most common form of haunting and there are many recorded in the county of Surrey. Not all are seen dressed in grey or wearing a monk's habit, a type of ghost whose authenticity we should perhaps be wary of! Well-known examples of apparitions detailed in this book include the ghost of the racing driver, Percy Lambert. He perished in a crash on the famous Brooklands track near Weybridge in 1913. Percy, dressed in racing cap and goggles, has been seen on a number of occasions strolling through the place of his greatest triumphs. But for the first time the true circumstances of his tragic demise are also told in *The Death of Percy Lambert*.

An apparition was also seen at Ash Manor in the 1930s, but this was linked to another commonly reported type of haunting — that of footsteps heard where no living person walks. The story is told in *The Prisoner*, showing that ghosts are also capable of making other sounds as well. The noise experienced in *Whistling in the Dark* is obvious, while the tolling of a bell was heard in *The Mystery of Haroldslea*. At Wotton House, near Dorking, the apparitions there may be connected with a room which remains particularly cold, even on the warmest days. Cold spots are another regularly reported ghostly phenomena.

Inexplicable visitations when the sleeper awakes in the middle of the night can be particularly disturbing. The sensation of 'something' on the end of the bed has been experienced by many Surrey people, and two examples are detailed in this book. This includes the strange case of *The Moodiwarp*, made public, I believe, for the first time.

At the moment of death the sufferer may appear to someone, often a loved one or friend, many miles away. The case of Lord Lyttleton is famous and cannot be omitted from any book of Surrey ghosts. A possibly less well known example from the county is detailed in *Death on a Train*. Sometimes such visions may reappear time and again, as happened in *The Secret of Welcomes Farm*.

Sometimes entire scenes of past tragedy have been re-enacted, as was the case in *An Incident at Hindhead* and *Take Me Home*. *Poltergeist at the Percy Arms* details a good example of another commonly reported but invisible ghost, who make their presence known by throwing objects about the place.

I hope that the Surrey hauntings selected here are a representative cross-section of the county's many ghosts, both in character and place. In some cases it has been necessary to reconstruct situations and speech based on the limited original information available. At all times the aim has been to provide the reader with firsthand evidence of the 'Ghosts of Surrey'.

John Janaway
September 1991

1

Whistling in the Dark

THE day that June and John Townsend moved into their new house near Godstone was a day that fulfilled their dreams. The noise and traffic fumes of main road suburban Norbury had become too much and they longed for the peace and tranquillity of the green countryside of Surrey.

It was an exciting time for both — there was new furniture to be bought, carpets and colour schemes to be chosen. But above all there was the planning of their brand new garden, for both were keen gardeners, frustrated by the pokey dark patch at the back of their former home in South London.

Once settled in to their new home, the Townsends quickly set about transforming what had been rough land adjacent to a farmyard into the garden of their dreams. Turf was laid, rockeries constructed and flower beds prepared for the summer plants. Although some of the planting had to take the turn of the seasons, by late spring the garden already looked like something to be proud of. It was much admired by their new neighbours including one who would come whistling along their quiet new road late in the evening and stop in front of John's fresh-built garden wall, perhaps to smell the scent of the flowers, the Townsends thought. But when they peered curiously from behind their living room curtains, the admirer of their horticultural efforts was nowhere to be seen.

As the weeks of a warm, balmy summer went by, the attentions of their whistling nocturnal visitor grew more regular. At times it sounded almost as if he was actually in their garden. Although they never saw him, his comforting whistle seemed to ward off the thoughts that sometimes entered the Townsends' minds. After all, we all whistle in the dark to give us confidence, to ward off any evil spirits which might be lurking, ready to waylay us, bringing cold and clammy terror.

However, no matter how hard they tried, a feeling of apprehension did begin to intrude upon their cosy lives whenever the tuneless whistling came near. Sometimes they heard the sound of his heavy boots definitely coming up the garden path and almost to their door. There could be no doubt about it. The Townsends began to pay more evening visits to the pub down the road 'Because we had made a lot of new friends and it was fun meeting them all down there', they said. But in their heart of hearts they knew the dream of their new home was turning sour and they had no wish to hear their whistling visitor any more. They mentioned it to nobody. Perhaps it was a vindictive neighbour who smiled at them in daylight but cursed them in the dark. It seemed far-fetched but had to be true. The next time they heard him, they would come out into their garden and have stern words to say.

And so it happened that one dark, moonless night in early winter, when the heavy footfalls came from the distance and the whistling started up, the Townsends were ready for a confrontation. This time the clump of heavy boots came right past the living room window, right through John's wallflower beds. The whistling invaded the peaceful house, echoing from wall to wall with a strange resonance, sounding as if the whistler was in every room at once.

'Curse the man!' John exclaimed, donning his coat as he did so. 'I've had enough of this!' June followed quickly behind her husband as he grabbed a torch from the kitchen drawer and rushed to the front door. As he opened the door the sounds of their nocturnal visitor ceased. Outside, although the weatherman had forecast an unusually mild night, the air was frosty cold. There was no moon and not even the hint of a breath of wind. John walked along the edge of his manicured lawn outside the living room window. It had rained a little during the afternoon and, as John shone the beam of his torch back and forth across the soft earth of the flower beds, he expected to see trampled plants and footmarks in the soft, damp soil. The shaft of light found only rows of healthy plants and undisturbed dark brown earth.

Just then an icy cold breeze got up and the whistling started again. The clump of boots came ever closer to the now terrified couple, but nothing could be seen. The increasing wind froze them to the marrow and ever, ever closer it came on. The now familiar sounds were accompanied by a metallic clang, like someone knocking the side of a bucket. On and on it came. It was right on top of them now. The whistling was now so loud that it seemed to be inside their heads. Clammy and cold, something, an invisible force, brushed past them, touching their faces. Then the sound and the wind died away as it passed down the side of the house and into the back garden.

The Townsends stood terrified and transfixed until the temperature began to rise and the mild evening came back to their now peaceful garden.

It was John who broke the silence. 'We need a drink,' he whispered to his white-faced wife. Without saying a further word, they walked mechanically down the road to the warmth and friendship of the pub.

'Two double brandies, please,' John stuttered.

'What's the trouble. You two look as if you've seen a ghost,' said the barman.

'Perhaps we have,' mumbled June, as with shaking hands she sipped her warming drink.

'Where?' asked a friendly local, only half smiling.

Then their story was told. The smiling faces of several regulars gradually changed to looks of serious thought.

'Ah! I've often wondered if Jim still walked,' said one, sucking hard upon his pipe. 'It must be over fifty year ago, when I was still young,' he continued with a twinkle in his eye. 'See, they knocked down the old farm to build those houses. There was this cowman, Jim was his name. Every evenin' he would draw water from the farm well, 'cept one night when he fell in instead. Found him drowned at the bottom next mornin' they did. Funny, really, because he was very superstitious, always whistled wherever he went to frighten away the nasties, he used to say. We used to call him 'Whistlin' Jimmy'. Always used to wear a crucifix around his neck, as extra insurance. Quite large this crucifix was and supposed to be quite valuable. Left to him by some aunt, I think. Funny, really, him goin' like that.

14

Mind you, there was some talk of murder at the time 'cos the crucifix was missin' when they pulled his body out of the well next day. But I reckon it had just come off when he fell and dropped into the ooze at the bottom.'

'Where was this well?' asked John, a solution to their problem, just a possibility, already forming in his mind.

'Now, let's see . . . Ah! Yes, I know. There's still a bit of the old farmyard wall at the bottom of your garden. It was just a yard or two in from there, in line with the old oak tree.'

John now knew what he had to do. Next morning, with surprisingly little difficulty, he located the well. It had been filled in with bricks and rubble. It took many hours of back-breaking work to clear it out but, with the help of two friends, he reached the bottom mud. Fortunately for John, the lowered water table and a dry summer meant the bottom was just a claggy ooze. He began to dig around with a garden fork. Bits of bucket, a few more bricks and two stoneware ginger beer bottles were soon retrieved. More bricks, more buckets and bits of sodden wood. It was beginning to get quite wet now. It must be here, it must! And suddenly there it was — fresh and gleaming in the dim light, looking as good as when Jimmy fell in — the crucifix.

With trembling hands John wiped it clean and climbed his ladder to the top of the well. In the rapidly fading evening light he placed the crucifix gently on the grass and went indoors.

Later on that night Jimmy came again, his boots thumping across the unmarked flower beds and lawn, his monotonous whistle shrill as usual. John and June went to bed more relaxed than they had been for months. John was sure it would be all right.

Next morning he was up early. He dressed quickly and

15

went out into the cold frosty dawn. There was the well, surrounded by piles of rubble and, there, marked out by the frost on the grass, was the spot where he had placed the crucifix the night before. The crucifix itself had gone. John smiled as a feeling of intense peace came over him. He knew that Whistling Jimmy would not return again.

2

Death on a Train

I AM unable to give the names of the two men involved in the story I am about to relate, but I can say that one of them rose to a high position in the country's judiciary. For his own reasons, which perhaps we can understand, he always insisted that his name should not be disclosed. Indeed, so well was his wish complied with that, as the years passed, his link with these events became completely severed and is unknown to the present writer.

The story begins at a well-known public school in the late years of the last century. Two pupils at the school, of similar background and mirror-like interests, became close and everlasting friends. They did everything together and even spent their holidays together. Such was the strength of their friendship that they formed a pact, a special secret society of theirs alone, to which no other could gain admittance. In order to seal this pact they made a cut in each other's arms and signed a secret paper with their blood. This paper contained a promise which one of them would eventually fulfil.

The boys remained inseparable until that momentous day eventually arrived — their last day at school. Amid great sorrow and with the promise that they would write, the two youths went their separate ways. One went up to university to follow a career in law while the other kept up the family tradition of joining the Indian Army.

At the beginning, when both were still in England, they did write to each other regularly — twice a day. But it was not long before it became once a day, then twice a week, then once a week. When the physical separation became the thousands of miles between London and India the correspondence faltered further until it finally ceased altogether. Both were successful in their chosen careers and found new companions and interests which eventually broke the friendship completely. The eminent barrister did maintain a tenuous link via the passing acquaintance of the brother of his erstwhile friend.

Many years passed until one Saturday not long before Christmas when the barrister decided to take a short break in the country. He needed to get away from the smoke of London and the strain of some particularly taxing cases in which he had been involved. So the following day he booked in at the Wheatsheaf Inn at Virginia Water, within a stone's throw of the lake of that name on the edge of Windsor Great Park.

After an excellent and relaxing dinner that evening, he sat in front of the fire smoking a soothing pipe of his favourite tobacco. Just at the moment when he should have been at his most relaxed, with the stresses of work put far behind, a strange feeling of unease and restlessness came over him. He could not explain the tension of his senses and remained sucking at his pipe for several minutes in an attempt to restore his well-being. But it was not to be.

18

Eventually, wrestling with his thoughts, he turned to the window where, much to his surprise, he fancied he saw a face peering in, staring at him from the dark beyond. The face he saw was uncannily familiar but he could not put a name to it. His unease continued and, pretending to go to the gas bracket on the wall to relight his pipe, he walked very slowly past the window, glancing out as he did so. There was definitely someone out there, someone whom he was sure he knew. But who? He could not remember. Once again he walked past the window and again he saw that face peering in at him. Who on earth was it? He sat down by the fire again, wracking his brains.

Filled with uncertainty and almost sick with unease he called the landlord. 'I think that there's a man spying at the window,' he said to his friendly host.

The landlord walked to the window, pressing his face almost to the glass. 'I don't think so, sir, I can't see anyone there,' he said, shaking his head. 'We lock the yard gate at ten o'clock so there won't be anybody out there at this time of night,' he assured the troubled barrister.

But the barrister was not satisfied, having convinced himself that there was someone or something outside. He resolved to investigate. 'I need some fresh air,' he told the landlord.

'I wouldn't go out, sir,' came the reply. 'There's a freezing east wind got up and it'll cut right through you.'

'But it's stifling in here and I must go out,' he insisted.

Outside the inn the night was pitch black and impenetrable. The barrister shuddered at the door before stepping out to face the icy wind. He stood shivering for a moment. There was no one there but then a very strange thing happened. Gradually the intensity of the darkness immediately in front of him seemed to become

19

concentrated in one place, like the entrance to a tunnel. After a while there came from the depths of that tunnel the vision of a train, the fiery glare of the engine fixed upon the night. As this vision became focused he could see the bright lights of the carriages and, in one of those carriages two men were locked in deadly combat.

One had hold of the other and appeared to be pushing him back towards the door of the carriage. Suddenly, as his assailant forced him against the door, it sprung open, and the man fell out. The barrister gazed in wide-eyed horror as the unfortunate man fell, face up, right at his feet, there in the yard of the Wheatsheaf Inn. The face stared up at him. It was the face he had seen at the window. Suddenly it dawned on him — it was the face of someone he had not seen since the days of his youth, the mature image of his once devoted friend of his school days. A friend to whom he had vowed eternal friendship sealed with their blood.

It was but a moment's vision which lasted an age. The barrister stood, petrified with shock and then it vanished. He screamed in horror and staggered back into the inn. He could not stay here another moment. He must get back to town that night. He still had time to catch the last train and this he did, arriving home very late and exhausted. But strangely the vision of that evening did not disturb his sleep and he awoke next morning feeling quite refreshed.

He busied himself in work for most of that Monday but late in the afternoon he decided to take a stroll. When he was in Piccadilly he saw his lost friend's brother and crossed the street to speak to him. This chance meeting instantly revived his memories of that terrible vision of the night before. The man looked pale and shocked when the barrister asked how his brother was getting on in India.

'It's very bad news,' he said with faltering voice. 'My brother's been killed, possibly murdered.'

'Could it be that he was thrown out of a railway carriage?' enquired the anxious barrister.

'Yes, yes, that's true, but how could you know? We only received the telegram this morning?'

Both stood in shocked silence, oblivious to the rattle of the traffic around them. The barrister remembered that secret paper sealing their pact in blood. He could see it now as clear as if it were yesterday. In his mind's eye he read the words scrawled on that paper before him: 'Whoever of us dies first must promise to appear to the other at the moment of death.' His friend had kept that promise in a peaceful corner of Surrey, thousands of miles from the place of his tragic end.

3

The Ghost of Ganghill

Mr and Mrs Fairweather lived for twenty years in a council house in Merrow, near Guildford. There seemed nothing extraordinary about the house — three-bedroomed and built in the early 1950s, a modern comfortable home where a family could be raised. It was not the sort of place you would have thought would be haunted. But haunted it was. There was a presence — an uneasy feeling at first which, as the years went by and the Fairweathers brought up their four children, became a terrible evil which brought misery to all the family. When it was there in the room it was like 'paralysis from the waist upwards' to Mrs Fairweather. Sometimes she felt herself pinned in bed by something which made the room go cold. That 'something' was often near her but never visible to her, and it would not go away.

It was her son who saw it — a man dressed in old-fashioned clothes, a long coat and a black hat. A sinister figure of menace, standing there in the cold room and then gone. The Fairweathers had moved to the house in Finches Rise in the 1950s. Twenty years later they thought only of moving as the activities of their uninvited guest reached a peak. None of the family would go upstairs alone. Small objects like watches were moved or went missing and always there was the sudden chill. 'You have to fight it or it won't leave you alone', said Mrs Fairweather. Her husband often used a bath towel to fight it off. 'Most nights he is up in the bedrooms, swishing a towel about to get rid of the thing.' The family brought in two priests to exorcise the ghost but to no avail.

By 1977, the household consisted of Mr and Mrs Fairweather, their married daughter, her husband and their two children. The ghost seemed particularly attracted to the young children.

Matters came to a head one terrible night in late May — a night the Fairweathers will never forget. It was Wednesday evening and there was a fearful storm. The air hung heavy, and the blue-black sky cracked and rumbled, while lightning forked and flashed, incandescent behind the neat roofs of lines of cosy houses, reaching down for the spire of Merrow church half a mile away. Not surprisingly, young Jamie was reluctant to go to bed but he was eventually persuaded. He seemed asleep while the thunder trampled back and forth across the dark and light of the evening sky.

Then came the child's shrill scream, piercing with terror. 'That's not my daddy!' the child cried. 'That's not my daddy, take him away!' he screamed yet again. What had the child seen — a tall man in a long coat wearing a black hat? Was it the sight of a deformed and twisted face which brought that horrendous scream? Grabbing the child, the family retreated downstairs to the front room, where the rest of the night was spent huddled together petrified with fear. Something had to be done.

The police were called and later that week *The Surrey Advertiser* reported the Fairweather's frightening story. The family just had to get away. 'We will accept anything, move anywhere,' said Mrs Fairweather. 'Anybody, anybody at all who can help us, please contact me — now this thing has grabbed my grandchild I am determined to get something done,' she appealed.

But why should such evil and terror haunt such an ordinary house, a house like thousands throughout Surrey? Now that the Fairweather's fearful experience was public news the researchers began to delve. Perhaps, when the reason was found, the ghost would be laid to rest and peace return to Finches Rise.

The answer seemed to lie in a small pamphlet found mouldering in the archives of Surrey Archaeological Society at Castle Arch in Guildford. Finches Rise had been built on what had been part of Ganghill Common, where the high gibbet once cast its grisly shadow and bodies swung silently in the summer breeze. The pamphlet described the execution of three 'malefactors' on the common. The date was Monday, 26th August 1776. The story of that day and the events leading up to it are preserved in the small print of this dog-eared scrap of paper.

James Potter, Frederick Gregg and Christopher Ellis had been convicted of robbery at the recent Assize. Now the cart drew them towards their fate on a summer morning on crowded Ganghill Common. Further crowds of the curious followed the slow moving procession, fascinated at the prospect of firsthand death.

James Potter was a young man, 'born of honest parents', who had once had the job of driving chaises or carriages to and from the White Hart, one of Guildford's fine High Street inns. But greed drove him to seek more than his simple wage could provide and he took to highway robbery. Astride his roan horse, pistol in hand, he held up William Calvert and two ladies on the wild downs of Banstead, relieving them of eleven guineas, a watch and some silver. He was arrested in Guildford while trying to dispose of some of his booty.

Frederick Gregg was found guilty of assaulting Allington Hodges on the highway, 'putting him in fear, and taking from his person, a metal watch'.

Finally, there was Christopher Ellis, found guilty of burglary. Ellis broke into the house of Elizabeth Binfield and stole two gold rings, a silver milk pot, a painted short silk apron, a muslin apron, a looking glass in a carved and gilt frame, five pounds in money and 'divers other goods'. Ellis was a tall man, frightening to look at and 'very much disfigured in the face, by having lost his nose'. A man ridiculed and rejected by his fellows, driven by spite and revenge. A man who might, perhaps, return even after death to taunt the innocent and make happy lives a dark misery.

Such were the crimes that brought these three men to the gallows on Ganghill Common. The procession reached its end about eleven o'clock. The accompanying minister then lead the three in prayer and they continued thus for nearly half an hour. Gregg was particularly penitent. 'I beg all young men to avoid bad women,' he declared, 'for that brought me to this shameful death. On behalf of all three of us, I want to thank the minister for his attendance upon us,' he continued. 'The minister has been a great comfort to us, treating us like his own children, and taking great pains to instruct us in the true principles of religion. I want to thank all those in the town of Guildford who have favoured us. We are all very sorry for what we have done,' he ended.

Standing on the specially made platform at the back of the cart, now positioned under the gallows, the ropes were placed around their necks. 'Lord have mercy on our souls!' they cried, as the cart was driven away and the three swung by the neck and rope on the journey beyond life.

But did Christopher Ellis, at least, return to the place of his death on the once bare and isolated Ganghill Common, his peace now broken by the living? Disfigured and tormented in death as in life, he seems to have selected the Fairweather family as victims for revenge. When a considerate council rehoused the family he went away and quiet normality returned to Finches Rise.

4

Two Sisters of Tadworth Court

TADWORTH Court, near Banstead, is a fine mansion built in about 1700. Since 1927 it has housed the well-known country branch of the Hospital for Sick Children. It is also home to a ghostly legend of jealousy, murder and suicide.

On one wall of the fine staircase which leads up from the main entrance there hangs a painting. A woman stands amongst fruit trees. Her right arm is outstretched and behind her is a basket already filled with juicy produce. A pleasant scene, one might think. But, over her left shoulder a sinister face peers out from between the branches of a tree. This weird image does not appear to be part of the picture as the artist intended. It is said that when first painted there was nothing behind the tree and that the face materialised following a horrible tragedy which befell the main subject of the painting.

Two sisters who lived at Tadworth Court were both in

love. Unfortunately their respective passions were directed at the same handsome young man. For his part he loved the sister whose portrait had recently been painted. The other sister seethed with a jealousy which drove her mad.

One day the young man arrived to visit his betrothed. She was upstairs and, on hearing him come through the main entrance of the house, she rushed from her bedroom onto the landing and leaned over the gallery to greet him. The other sister also came out onto the landing. When she saw the happy smiles exchanged by the two lovers, all reason snapped. Wild eyed, she grabbed her sister from behind and pitched her over the banister. With a terrible scream, which echoed throughout the house, her sister plummeted to the stone floor below. The fall killed her instantly.

Stunned momentarily into sanity by the sight of her sister's blood oozing across the flagstones, the murderess ran back through her bedroom and into a dressing room opening off it. She then climbed a small staircase and went out onto the roof. Once there she quickly ended her own life by hurling herself to the ground below.

Within a few days of this tragedy, when the family could bring themselves to look upon the portrait of their dear departed daughter again, they noticed with horror that the other sister's image had appeared within a space behind the trees.

It is said that when the picture was removed, the sisters returned to re-enact their deaths. Once more that terrible scream was heard in the house, then came the dull thud upon the stone floor and the flow of blood which refused to be wiped away. And so the picture was returned to its usual place on the grand staircase and the flagstones, where death came instantly, were torn up and replaced.

The haunting of Tadworth Court is a good story in the best tradition but are there any pegs of truth upon which to hang the cloak of legend? In 1928 a well-researched book on the history of the house was published. The author was Frances Leaning and she went to great lengths to try to find some elements of fact about a legend known to almost everyone in Tadworth.

Firstly she searched the documentary records for the violent deaths of the two sisters but found nothing. All the children of the families who had lived there since 1700 were accounted for, and none had died in suspicious or unusual circumstances. That left only the painting. One thing she was certain of was that the style of the subject's clothing showed that she was not English. She also doubted if the portrait had been painted on English soil.

But what of that strange face peering from among the branches? The expert's verdict was that the canvas had been used twice — in other words the second picture had been painted on top of an earlier work. The face in the trees belonged to the original picture. Apparently it is not unusual for such painting to begin to show through after a number of years. Therefore, the verdict was that neither the documents nor the painting could support the authenticity of the ghostly legend.

How then would such a story originate and then be passed down through several generations of local people? The picture expert suggested to Frances Leaning that the legend could have originated from the painting itself. After all, it certainly does have mystery. Who was the woman in the orchard and who is hiding in the trees? A little imagination could soon conjure up a fine old yarn and, as the years passed, further embellishments would be sure to follow.

That then must put paid to the ghosts of Tadworth Court, or does it? On one occasion since the war the painting was removed for cleaning. Although during its absence no apparitions were seen falling to their past deaths, there was a series of what were described as 'domestic mishaps'. Matters became so bad that the return of the picture was urgently requested. And there it hangs to this day — the young woman's face implacable, the unpleasant impression of that watching figure behind her. It may be that together they have secrets no expert can discover.

5

The Death of Percy Lambert

'Hey, you, stop! Stop, I say!' yelled the security guard as the silent figure wandered off into the mist towards the river. But his words seemed not to penetrate the dank air. The guard walked quickly in the same direction, tracking the nocturnal trespasser, wondering what the man was doing here. A few yards further on and he could see the man no more. The dark figure had evaporated into the chill night air and vanished.

Who was he, this strange figure, so quaintly dressed in racing helmet and goggles? And where had he gone? In his heart the guard already knew the answer to the second question as he stood, shivering a little, peering into the foggy gloom beyond the aircraft factory buildings. The man he had seen was not of this world. He belonged to the unique history of this place and his name was Percy Lambert. This is his story.

The morning of Friday, 31st October 1913 dawned

heavy with mist and dampness, but by 9 o'clock it had cleared and a fine autumn day was in prospect. Percy Lambert, or 'Pearly' as he was known, sat ready at the wheel of his streamlined 25 h.p. Talbot racing car on the start line of Surrey's 'eighth wonder of the world' — Brooklands.

Brooklands Motor Course was the brainchild of a single-minded man dedicated to the motorcar. His name was Hugh Locke King and he lived in a large house near Weybridge station on the edge of St George's Hill. For generations his family had owned estates around Weybridge and the surrounding country. He was an instantly recognisable figure as he drove about the district in his large 'Itala'. Sometimes he took the car on extensive continental tours.

Locke King was particularly concerned that British car builders should be given every facility to develop vehicles as good as their counterparts in Europe. But, in the main, the British establishment was against the 'horseless carriage', limiting its speed on the open road to twenty miles per hour. In towns it was half that speed, and many local magistrates soon gained a reputation for the swingeing fines they imposed on those who dared to use the full power of their motors. Some Surrey towns, such as Godalming, were notorious among the motoring fraternity for the efficiency of their speed traps. The motor industries in France and Italy faced no such restrictions. Locke King recognised that the country needed a purpose-built track on private land, where cars could be tested and raced flat out for hour after hour without their drivers facing arrest.

Below St George's Hill, the Locke King Estate included a large tract of damp and marshy meadowland astride the meandering River Wey. The place was infested with rabbits and not much else. Locke King was determined that this was the spot where his motor track would be built. In 1906 plans were drawn up, and in eight months the area transformed. It was a colossal undertaking. At the height of the building, two thousand men were employed, working almost non-stop. The river was diverted and bridged in two places; massive concrete banking nearly thirty feet high constructed on the bends and 350,000 cubic yards of soil and sand excavated. At the north-east end of the course the track went through a cutting before emerging, steeply banked, to cross the River Wey. The natural hill here became known as Members' Hill and for a short distance it obscured the track from spectators in the finishing straight. Members' Bridge crossed the track at the north end of the hill.

Brooklands Motor Course was officially opened on 17th June 1907. In just a few short months peaceful meadow had been turned into two and three-quarter miles of oval, 100-foot wide, concrete track, with a separate finishing straight in the middle. This giant arena, with the spectacular banking of its bends, awaited the combat of its motorised gladiators.

However, the first meeting, held on 6th July 1907, was not a great success. The races were difficult to follow, mainly because the cars raced without numbers. Spectators were expected to identify them by means of the racing colours worn by the drivers, rather like jockeys. This similarity to horse racing extended to entry fees and prize money, which were given in sovereigns, while the results of each race were put up on a board just like those still seen today at Sandown, just a few miles from Brooklands. The official starter just happened to be a member of the Jockey

Club. Modern motor racing tracks still have a paddock, but the first one was at Brooklands.

However, once the problems had been ironed out, the crowds began to flock to see this exciting new spectator sport. The track also became very popular with drivers and car makers seeking speed and endurance records. By October 1913, many of the drivers had become public heroes, none more so than the 32 year old record breaker, Percy Lambert.

The previous February he had become the first driver in the world to cover 100 miles in an hour. But now the record stood at 107.95 m.p.h. and was held by a Frenchman, Jean Chassagne, driving a Sunbeam. Percy Lambert was anxious to regain the record before the year was out.

Motor racing was his life, and he had been here many times before, feeling the tingling anticipation of the exhilaration ahead, resolute in his determination to beat the world record. Percy was a dedicated man — he always trained to peak fitness for his record attempts. He never drank alcohol and very seldom smoked. Since 7 o'clock that morning he had waited patiently for the sun to lift the clammy vapours of an October night. He was confident that his massive machine, with its 4,754 c.c., four cylinder engine and weighing well over a ton, would soon regain the prize for his sponsor, Lord Shrewsbury.

Tyres were always a problem in the early days of speed. The technology of the pneumatic tyre had lagged behind the rapid progress made by engine designers. On the previous Monday Percy Lambert had been lucky when a tyre on his Talbot had burst. For this fresh attempt on the record a set of brand new Palmer cord tyres had been fitted to the steel rims on the wood-spoked wheels. As an extra special precaution, about a dozen security bolts were fixed to each of them to prevent any chance of the tyres moving on their rims. No detail had been left unconsidered — the car had been thoroughly checked in every detail. Percy and his mechanics were totally confident that the Frenchman's record would fall.

At 9.20 the Talbot scorched from the start line, the thump and thunder of its massive four cylinders soon blending into an ear-splitting roar, the helmeted driver, goggles down, hunched over the huge steering wheel.

All was going to plan — the Talbot hurtling round, high on the banking, with metronomic regularity. Among the spectators was William Macintyre, son of one of the Brooklands lodgekeepers, who had come to watch from the safety of the Members' Bridge. After about half an hour, the Talbot had completed twenty laps of the track at an average speed of 110.4 m.p.h. A split second after disappearing from view behind Members' Hill, while three quarters of the way round the twenty first lap, there was a loud bang. The eerie silence that followed was long enough for Major Lindsay Lloyd, Clerk of the Course, who was timing Lambert, to remark to a companion 'He has burst another tyre'. The silence was then broken by a 'horrible clatter', which told all those present that there had been a terrible accident.

Meanwhile, William Macintyre, from his vantage point on the bridge, had seen the fate of Percy Lambert unfold almost beneath his feet.

'As Mr Lambert came round the bend behind the hill, travelling to the top of the bank, one of his tyres burst', Macintyre reported. 'He swerved half-way down the bank and then resumed a straight course at a somewhat reduced speed. The car travelled irregularly for about fifty yards, and then turned upwards and got on top of the bank, the off-side wheels going over the cement on to the sand on the other side.'

Macintyre was witnessing a driver struggling for his life, wrestling with a writhing monster on a wall of death.

'After travelling in this position a very little distance, the car turned turtle,' Macintyre continued. 'It then began to roll over and over down the cement'. Percy Lambert had lost the struggle.

'After the second roll I saw Mr Lambert lying on the track.'

Those who rushed to the scene found Percy Lambert lying face down about half-way up the banking. He was unconscious but still breathing. The car was standing upright against the brickwork of the bridge; the remains of the burst offside rear tyre were about ten or fifteen yards away. Percy Lambert was rushed to Weybridge Cottage Hospital in Brooklands' own ambulance, but all life was extinguished during the few minutes of the journey.

The mortal remains of Percy Lambert, who had lived in Knightsbridge, were buried in Brompton Cemetery, a spoked wheel marking his grave. It was suggested at the inquest on the day following his death that, had he succeeded in this record attempt, he intended to retire from record breaking. But records were Percy Lambert's goal in life and perhaps in death too, for it was not long before stories began to circulate of a ghostly figure, with racing helmet and goggles, seen walking along the track. There were reports also of the sound of the 25 h.p. Talbot as it roared invisibly around Brooklands' massive banking. It was even claimed that the car itself had been seen, Percy Lambert at the wheel. It travelled for about a hundred feet and then vanished.

The spot where Percy Lambert died by Members' Bridge

is still recognisable today. That this place is haunted, there can be no doubt. Test Hill, a very steep incline once used for cars, motorcycles and even bicycles runs up towards the track near the bridge. One night in the early 1970s a British Aircraft Corporation security man was looking across towards the hill, when he saw a large blob of 'blackness' floating above the area. Then he heard a terrible sound of 'crashing, splintering metal or wood. I was petrified to the extent that I could not move. Test Hill was still overgrown at that time, but two days later, when I plucked up courage to investigate, not a blade of grass, nor a branch of a tree had been broken,' he related sometime later.

'There is definitely something strange in that area, and I'm a level headed chap who doesn't imagine things,' he insisted.

Many people now agree that the haunting of that area must be related to the tragedy of an October day in 1913.

Following the First World War, Brooklands went from success to success, not just as a centre of motor racing, but also for motorcycles, bicycles and, of course, aircraft. In 1935 John Cobb in his giant 'Napier-Railton' with its 450 h.p., 12 cylinder, aero engine, raised the lap record to a staggering 143.44 m.p.h., a record which was never to be broken.

The onset of war in 1939 saw the end of racing at Brooklands as all activity was concentrated on aircraft production, which the great aviation pioneer, A. V. Roe, had initiated back in December 1907. During the war, hangars were built on the track and part of the embankment dug away. The story of the Brooklands Motor Course was at an end, or was it?

Very recently Brooklands has been undergoing another transformation. The aircraft factory, famous for the

Wellington bomber, the Vickers Viscount and much more besides, has been flattened. New industrial enterprises are rising from its rubble, but the heyday of the place has not been forgotten. Brooklands Museum, tracing all aspects of a unique history, has been opened using the old clubhouse as its centre. Substantial parts of the famous banking have survived, and where Percy Lambert lost his life his spirit lingers, still seeking a record that is really his.

6

Merry Hall

THE writer, composer, garden and cat lover Beverley Nichols, who died in 1983, lived for some years in a fine Georgian mansion at Ashtead called Merry Hall. One of his books, *Up the Garden Path*, is a description of his garden there. Nichols, who firmly claimed to believe in ghosts, related a fascinating tale of the haunting of his house in another of his books, *Laughter on the Stairs*. Nichols was adamant that his story was true. 'If you think that this is just another piece of whimsey you can look it up in the reference books. I did myself,' he wrote. Certainly some of the facts upon which it was based can be verified, even though he failed to record them accurately.

The story concerns a previous owner of Merry Hall and a horse of his which won the Grand National. According to Nichols the horse was called *Ilex* and his owner was Mr J. C. Masterman. Nichols further asserted that the horse had won the National in 1893 and had been bred at Merry Hall.

Nichols claimed to have learnt many of the facts of the story from an old man who had called to do odd jobs in the garden. The man had worked there as a boy nearly sixty years before, when Masterman owned the house. He said that Masterman had a passion for the horses he owned 'that passed the bounds of reason'. His horses were kept at Merry Hall under the care of an old groom called Withers. In company with his groom, Masterman would spend hours with his horses, both night and day, sometimes sitting among the straw with a bottle of champagne, talking to them.

When *Ilex* won the Grand National the excitement proved too much for Masterman's constitution. He took to his bed and within a few weeks he was dead. The day he died Withers got out his beloved horses and led them up and down in front of the window, for Masterman to see them for the final time.

The haunting at Merry Hall was experienced not by Beverley Nichols himself but by a visiting friend whom he called 'Miss Mint'. It was late October, a Sunday, and Miss Mint was expected at Merry Hall for supper. She was to arrive by bus, having refused the offer of a lift by car. The bus stopped in Ashtead village some way short of her destination, but Miss Mint was determined that she would walk the rest of the way. It would only take ten minutes at the most.

It was a clear October evening as darkness fell, with perhaps a suggestion of frost; the moon was nearly full. Beverley Nichols busied himself preparing for his visitor, decorating the house with small arrangements of flowers. About half past six he heard a strange noise, 'a curious sliding sound', at the front door. Plucking up his courage, Nichols flung open the door to find Miss Mint half kneeling on the doorstep and about to faint.

When she had recovered, Miss Mint was totally

40

convinced that she had seen a ghost and Nichols did not doubt her. She had got off the bus in the village at just before six o'clock and set out for the short walk to Merry Hall. Nichols noted that the walk had actually taken her half an hour. She had not been waiting at the door for twenty minutes, so what had happened to that missing time?

Miss Mint claimed to have walked into the past! She had realised something was wrong, she said, when, as she approached Merry Hall, she saw in the distance a line of large elm trees, which she knew were no longer there. Nichols had had them cut down sometime before. And then the layout of some of the buildings was different and the modern garage was not there.

Miss Mint came to a five-barred gate. A very short, foxy faced man wearing breeches was leaning over the gate. He greeted her in a voice which sounded like an echo. He asked if she was going to Merry Hall. When she said yes, he referred to a 'sad business'. He then described how the horses had been got out of the stables early that morning to be paraded past his master's bedroom window for the last time. Miss Mint's words exactly fitted the facts that Nichols knew of Masterman's last hours back in 1893.

Nichols had an old map dated 1895, and he was able to trace the positions of Masterman's old stables in the exact place Miss Mint had described. And there was the position of the five-barred gate right where she had met the little man in breeches!

To confirm Miss Mint's experience he recalled an incident involving one of his beloved cats a week before. The cat, 'One' (his four cats were named from one to four), had taken fright whilst Nichols was carrying him down the driveway. 'One' had leapt from his arms, wailing, staring at something straight ahead and refusing to go further. Finally, the cat jumped high in the air as if vaulting over an invisible gate. It was precisely where the old five-bar gate had been!

Such are the 'facts' of Beverley Nichols' story, but do any real facts support its authenticity? That a horse called *Ilex* did win the Grand National cannot be disputed, nor that he was owned by a Mr Masterman, who had indeed lived at Merry Hall in the 1890s. But *Ilex* won the race in 1890 not 1893, for Mr George not 'J. C.' Masterman, who was a well-known figure in Ashtead and Epsom. He appears to have bought Merry Hall in the late 1870s.

The origins of *Ilex* are interesting, although not in keeping with the Nichols' version. The story starts before George Masterman owned the horse. The famous National Hunt jockey, Arthur Nightingale, was engaged to ride *Ilex* as a four year old in a selling race at Leicester in 1888. Where *Ilex* was bred is not recorded but it was certainly not at Merry Hall. Nightingale was a member of the famous Epsom based family of racehorse trainers. When he first saw the horse he was far from impressed. *Ilex* was a shaggy looking chestnut with a large belly and ominous looking bandages on his legs — often the sign of a horse with bad legs. On the way to the start the owner appeared on the scene and promptly removed these bandages, which had been merely an aid to obtaining longer odds! *Ilex* proceeded to win by a street's length, the jockey being so impressed that he persuaded George Masterman to buy him. The horse was then trained at Epsom by John Nightingale, the jockey's father.

Following his 1890 success, *Ilex* finished third in the Nationals of 1891 and 1892. In the latter race he broke down so badly that he never raced again. Maybe he was retired to Merry Hall.

George Masterman died in November 1897, rather too long after his National success to have been killed by the excitement. However, he had been ill at home for sometime before his death, so it is possible that *Ilex* was paraded past his bedroom window the day he died.

Perhaps too few ghost stories stand much close scrutiny, but such are the true facts of Beverley Nichols' story. Each of us must come to our own conclusions regarding its authenticity!

7

The Secret of Welcomes Farm

'I THINK, superintendent, that my son is dead.'

'I see, sir, and what makes you think so?' enquired Superintendent Carlin of Scotland Yard.

'I hope you won't think this silly, but my wife has had a vision.'

'I see, sir,' repeated the superintendent, trying to appear to be taking the situation seriously. 'Now, let's make sure I've got the details correct. You are the Reverend Gordon Tombe, is that right?'

'Yes, superintendent, and my son's name is . . .' and here he paused. 'Or was, I perhaps ought to say, Eric, George Eric Tombe, but he was always known by his second name.'

'Tomb, as in grave?' asked Carlin, with barely concealed amusement.

'No, superintendent, it has an 'e' at the end,' replied the Reverend Tombe with slight annoyance in his voice. He had long grown tired of that particular pun.

Sensing that, Carlin quickly moved the subject on. 'Where does your son live?'

'Until just over a year ago he lived at Welcomes Farm, Kenley.'

'And after that?'

'Well, I think he took some lodgings for a while after the fire. And then he just disappeared.'

'A fire, sir. Please tell me about it?' said Carlin, as he straightened up in his chair, his interest kindled.

'Eric has . . . or had, a passion for horses — it's not necessarily something I would ever encourage, you understand. Not long after the war he met up with this chap — I only met him once and I usually accept people until events prove otherwise. Now this chap, his name was Ernest Dyer, looked a dishonest type to me. Most unusually for me, I took an instant dislike to him. The two of them were set on buying a farm where they could breed and train racehorses. I wouldn't have tried to dissuade my son, superintendent, but I certainly wasn't happy with the situation.'

'Did your Eric know much about horses?' Carlin enquired.

'He could ride quite well but he hadn't any real experience of the business side of things,' the Reverend replied. 'Eric and Dyer managed to raise a great deal of money, five thousand pounds I believe, and they bought Welcomes Farm. It wasn't long before Eric realised that he was doing all the work. Matters came to a head only a few weeks after they moved into the farm when they had a flaming row. Dyer admitted to Eric that he wasn't really interested in horses and preferred racing cars. However, matters improved after that but a few weeks later, when Eric was up north, the farm was badly damaged in a fire.'

45

'I see,' mumbled Carlin who was now deep in thought. 'Please go on.'

'Eric knew that he was ruined. They'd skimped somewhat on the insurance, you see. But later he found out that Dyer had secretly insured the place for twelve thousand pounds, which he was going to claim entirely for himself. I think Eric just happened to be there when the insurance assessor arrived. Dyer tried to flannel but the truth was soon out. Unfortunately, the fact that the fire was now not such a disaster persuaded Eric not to be too hard on his scheming partner. For a few days it seemed as if matters would sort themselves out. With the insurance money they could rebuild the farm and make it into a really first-class establishment. But then the insurance company refused to pay up.'

'And why was that, sir?' Carlin enquired although he felt he already knew the answer.

'They said they thought the fire had been started deliberately.'

'That's very interesting. Perhaps there's something on our files about that. Now you say you think your son is dead. Why's that?'

'He's disappeared, just gone. He left no forwarding address. No one seems to know where Dyer's gone either. They've just vanished!'

'Couldn't they have run off because they thought they might be in trouble over the insurance business?' Carlin suggested.

'But Eric had nothing to do with it. He told me so and I know he was speaking the truth. He had no reason to run. He had nothing to hide,' insisted the Reverend Tombe. 'And then there's my wife's visions, dreams, call them what you like. She knows he's dead, superintendent, she's sure of it and I believe her.'

'Oh yes, sir,' said Carlin a little doubtfully.

'Superintendent, she can't sleep. The vision keeps coming to her night and day. I promised her that the police would do something — investigate to find out what has happened to our son,' he implored.

'What is this vision?' asked Carlin quietly, trying to sound sincere. He could at least understand a parent's worry over a lost son, even though the vision idea was too far-fetched for him. He dealt with facts, not dreams.

'She sees him lying there, contorted, dead. It comes to her in broad daylight. Her eyes are open and there is our son's body, his head all bloody, his eyes staring up at her. She says he seems to be at the bottom of a deep hole but she can't explain why — it's just a dark hole, damp and rounded. It might be a well. Please help us, superintendent, or I think my wife will go mad.'

The interview ended with Carlin telling the Reverend Tombe that 'they would look into it'. The superintendent was as good as his word, although he considered that it was, perhaps, a case of fraud they were dealing with rather than anything more sinister.

It was March 1920, not long after the Reverend's visit that police began to make enquiries regarding Ernest Dyer's business dealings. What they discovered confirmed Carlin's suspicions about the case. Dyer had been involved in a number of 'shady' deals. When they examined the books of Welcomes Farm they found that he had managed to embezzle nearly £3,000 from the accounts. The search was on to find Ernest Dyer.

They found him in July but, as is often the way in such

matters, the discovery was accidental — what the police would call 'a lucky break'. Police in Scarborough had been on the trail of a man called Fitzsimmons who had been passing dud cheques. They finally tracked him down to a hotel in the Yorkshire seaside resort. Fitzsimmons was armed and, when police tried to arrest him, there was a struggle which ended with Fitzsimmons being fatally wounded. Among the dead man's effects police found ample evidence that Fitzsimmons was, in fact, none other than Ernest Dyer. They also found about a hundred and eighty blank cheques all signed by an 'Eric Tombe'.

But where was George Eric Tombe? His mother continued to be haunted by the vision of her dead son. She saw his staring, lifeless eyes, his bloody head and she knew that the grave had claimed him, but where was that grave? Perhaps, the police thought, there might be something in it. Their efforts were now concentrated on the overgrown ruins of Welcomes Farm. The brambles and weeds were cleared away and an extensive and very detailed search made of the whole site. During their investigations the police discovered no less than five wells. The first two contained nothing that could assist them in finding the whereabouts of the missing man.

It was growing dark when they started their investigations of the third well. By the eerie wavering light of their lamps they continued their work in that slimy, dank hole until very late into the evening. It was shortly after midnight when some human remains were brought to the surface. They were all that was left of George Eric Tombe. He had been shot in the back of the head. His mother's vision had proved to be true but now it would come to her no more. It is probable that, at the very moment when the terrible image first appeared, Ernest Dyer was disposing of his erstwhile partner, her son. Without that vision the secret of Eric Tombe's disappearance would have remained sealed deep beneath the site of Welcomes Farm for ever.

8

The Camera Cannot Lie

O NE day in October 1962 the well-known local historian
of Thames Ditton, the late T. S. Mercer, paid a visit to
the Home of Compassion in his village. The house had
previously been known as Boyle Farm until it was bought
by the Church of England Community of the Compassion
of Jesus in 1905. 'Farm' is actually rather a misnomer for
the fine looking house originally built in 1786 for Charlotte
Boyle Walsingham. Although much altered since, it still
has an imposing brick edifice with grounds leading down
to the banks of the River Thames.

T. S. Mercer had come armed with his camera to
photograph some murals which workmen had just
uncovered during redecoration of a room which, until
1925, had served as the Home's chapel. The room must
have once looked quite inspiring. It was decorated with a
mosaic of the Lord's Supper over the altar, with two smaller
mosaics of St Peter and the Angel Gabriel either side of it.

Around the walls were the skilfully painted murals. They consisted of four large panels depicting the saints but with further decoration which covered both walls and ceiling. The painting was the work of one of the members of the community, Sister Miriam, who was still alive, aged about 85, and living in Kent at the time of Mercer's visit.

Unfortunately, although examples of Sister Miriam's work survived elsewhere in the Home, these murals had presumably been painted over when a separate brick chapel, connected to the main house by cloisters, had been built. The passing of time and the over-painting had not served the murals well. It was not intended that they should remain exposed, so the Rev Mother Superior gave the popular local historian permission to record them. Soon after, they disappeared from view once more beneath layers of fresh paint.

When Mercer arrived the three decorators at work in the room downed their scrapers and brushes to watch as he took his photographs. He took five in all. Everything seemed perfectly normal to the four people present. The job done, Mercer packed away his camera, no doubt giving his thanks for this fortunate opportunity, and departed pleased that another little bit of his village's history had been recorded for posterity. He did not realise that something else, unseen by the human eye, had also been captured in the camera's lens.

When his photographs were developed four of them had come out perfectly, but it was the fifth which caused the most interest and curiosity. Something had passed before the camera, leaving a white and wispy image which partially obscured the intended subject. The 'something' curved from the bottom right to the top left of the photograph — a white vapour, veiled and ethereal. At first

Mercer thought nothing of it, considering it to be the result of a fault in the film or the processing. But information he received later caused him to look again at this strange photograph.

He learnt that Boyle Farm had a long history of hauntings. Spectral figures, vaguely transparent like that in his picture, had been seen by the nurses, patients and helpers. One regular visitor to the home often brought her dog. On several occasions the dog would suddenly start to growl and his fur bristle at an unseen source of distress. And then the dog's owner saw a ghostly figure in white walking the corridors to disappear before her eyes. Such was the level of ghostly activity in one particular room that it was kept locked for many years. After it was reopened, a strange presence still stalked the room. For three days in succession Holy Communion was held there in an attempt to exorcise the ghost, but to no avail. Could Mercer's photograph have captured one of Boyle Farm's restless spirits, he pondered?

The first thing to do was to have the photograph and its negative checked by an expert. After careful study the expert declared that the unseen image captured by Mercer's camera could not have been the result of a defective film or faulty processing. He checked the camera and was equally sure that it had functioned perfectly. His conclusion was that something, perhaps a bright object, had definitely passed in front of the lens whilst the shutter was open. But what or who? Did the history of Boyle Farm hold any clues to the persistent hauntings?

Thames Ditton almost owes its existence to the magnificent palace of Hampton Court. The park of Cardinal Wolsey's gift to Henry VIII lies opposite across the River Thames, and the roofs and chimneys of that vast building dominate the skyline. Here at 'Dytton uppon Tamys' court officials built their homes, away from the strictures and sometimes the dangers of Henry's court.

Boyle Farm was built on the site of an earlier house known as Forde's Farm, named after Erasmus Forde who owned it in the early 16th century. Forde Farm was bought by Charlotte Boyle Walsingham in 1782. Four years later, on 5th March 1786, she recorded in her diary: 'I laid the first stone of my new house — Boyle Farm'. Mrs Walsingham was quite a figure in society and a great friend of Horace Walpole. The house as originally built with crenellated roofline was certainly influenced by Walpole's house at Strawberry Hill.

Mrs Walsingham's daughter, Charlotte, married the actor, Lord Henry Fitzgerald, who in his time was considered as good at his profession as Garrick. Perhaps the most colourful figures connected with Boyle Farm were Henry's brother, Edward, and Edward's wife Pamela, known as 'La Belle Pamela'. Pamela had an eventful life but one much touched by tragedy. Edward was shot in Ireland while being arrested for supporting insurrection. Shortly afterwards, on 4th June 1798, he died in prison while awaiting trial for treason. His wife had been one of the most beautiful women at the court of Louis XVI. Her father was executed by guillotine during the French Revolution, while her half-brother later became King Louis-Phillipe, who ended his days in exile at Claremont near Esher.

Pamela made many happy visits to Boyle Farm but in her later years she led a sad life, wandering Europe with no fixed home and mounting debts. She died in Paris in 1831 and was buried in the cemetery at Montmartre. But that was not the end of her wanderings. During the siege of

Paris in 1870, a Prussian shell smashed her grave. Her remains were temporarily put into a vault in the same cemetery, but later her bones were brought to their final resting place in Thames Ditton churchyard. Her gravestone incorporates part of the original stone from Montmartre which was inscribed by the Duc de la Force with the words: 'Pamela Ladye Edward Fitzgerald par son ami le plus devoue L.L.' Perhaps it is 'La Belle Pamela' who walks the corridors of the Home of Compassion, drawn by the memory of happiness amidst a life of some tragedy.

The answer must always remain conjecture. But what is certain is that someone or something was in the room that day in October 1962. Invisible to the four people present, it passed before T. S. Mercer's camera to leave a permanent image which no normal reasoning can explain.

9

An Incident at Hindhead

ROBIN Brown is one of life's great eccentrics. A short, rather rotund man with a jovial, shiny face and a twinkle in his eye. Robin loves hats and is never seen without something made of cloth or felt covering his now thinning hair. Not that he's vain, I assure you, but he just feels undressed without a cap or trilby, depending upon the occasion. Look at an old photograph of a hundred years ago — groups of men, women and children stand without expression, flat-faced to the camera's telling eye, with not a bare head in sight. Well, Robin could be amongst that Victorian crowd and blend in perfectly. A man after his time is Robin Brown.

Robin walks with a slight limp, the result of a nasty accident he had some years ago. Early one morning two hikers found poor Robin halfway down the Devil's Punchbowl at Hindhead. He was in a terrible state and not too far from death it is said. His face was badly gashed but you won't see the scar now — it's hidden under his hat! But his worst injury was his leg, which was horribly smashed. It needed a steel plate and quite a few screws to put that right. But how did he come to be there? That was the mystery. He had left his bicycle at home when he went out the day before. There appeared to be no vehicle involved and no sign of a violent crash. Robin didn't drive. 'Can't stand those destructive, polluting things', he always says, although he is rarely adverse to the offer of a lift. So there was a puzzle, indeed, but he was always very reluctant to tell despite often being pressed to explain, so a mystery it remained. That is, until now.

Robin is an inveterate collector of almost everything — stamps, fossils, old books — you name it and he has a collection of it! His small flat in a rambling Victorian house is stuffed from top to bottom with what some of us might call junk. At the moment he has a fad for the labels off old beer bottles but he also collects the bottles too. Most of them are empty, of course. Robin also has a penchant for collecting the taste of fine ales from the barrel. I have spent many an entertaining evening with him at some remote hostelry or other savouring the latest brew.

Thus it was that one evening recently we found ourselves at the Prince of Wales at Hammer, on the borders where Hampshire, Sussex and Surrey meet. Perhaps it was the exceptional quality of the contents of his glass but I at last succeeded in prising from him the details of that day and night which so nearly ended in tragedy.

'We're not far from Hindhead,' I said as more of a question than a statement.

'Well, of course,' said Robin, holding his recently refilled glass to the light and minutely studying its rich brown glints. His nostrils twitched above the glass before he drank. He swallowed slowly, smacked his lips in satisfaction, then placed the glass deliberately and accurately upon the beermat in front of him on the table.

'O.K. I'll tell you but you must believe it's true,' he emphasized. 'And no laughing, because it wasn't funny, I can tell you.'

'Surely you know me better than to think I would treat your accident as a joke,' I replied with as much sincerity as I could muster.

Robin paused for a long time and lifted his glass for another mouthful of ale. He put the half empty glass down again and leant back in his chair. When Robin was going to explain things it was always essential that he had both hands free. 'You know that I've been rather interested in collecting old Victorian bottles for some years now. Well, I heard from a friend that there were some old rubbish dumps on Bramshott Common where somebody had found some Codd's bottles — you know, those things with the marble inside. So I decided to investigate. I planned it like an expedition of exploration, into the unknown and all that! I had my knapsack and folding shovel, thermos and sandwiches. I thought I'd make a day of it — do some walking and perhaps find a few old bottles if I was lucky.'

'I got the train from Milford to Haslemere rather later in the morning than I had originally intended,' he continued. 'I'm afraid the ale at the Anchor the previous evening had been rather flavoursome. I walked up Marley Lane and across Hindhead Common towards Gibbet Hill. I'm sure that spot must be haunted — the place where they hanged the three murderers of the 'unknown sailor' in 1786. They put the bodies in an iron cage and left them swinging there as a warning to others. There's those gory lines of that poem about it: Hanging there both night and day, till piece by piece they dropped away! Lovely!' he exclaimed, placing his empty glass firmly in front of me.

With glass refilled Robin continued his tale. 'From Gibbet Hill I made my way to the Hindhead crossroads. It had been a beautiful spring morning with just a little nip in the air, but on the hill I was disappointed to see clouds rolling up from the north-west. I continued my way along the footpath at the side of the road and headed towards Bramshott Common, cursing that I had forgotten my map and had to suffer the roar of constant traffic. The A3 at Bramshott was still only single carriageway then, not the wide double road it is now. I rambled round the common on both sides of the road and sat virtuously in a sheltered spot by a tree to eat my sandwiches and drink a cup of tea. After the previous night this day was going to be teetotal, I can tell you! I know when to stop,' he said emphatically.

'The sky was rapidly filling with clouds and a cold wind getting up, so I was pleased to find such a cosy spot. I then pressed on down the slope towards Waggoners Wells. For quite a while I walked up and down the wooded slopes, searching. Eventually I was lucky to find myself walking down a gully where I could see the unmistakable signs of a rubbish dump left by the military when this area was one vast army camp during the First World War. I was soon so pre-occupied searching around that I failed to notice the passing of time or the gathering darkness of thick rain clouds. I was brought down to earth, so to speak, when the heavens suddenly opened and drenching rain came down in sheets.'

'Time for home, I thought, as I packed up quickly and made my way back across the common towards the road. But I had forgotten the route I had taken and I have to confess that, at one point, I was quite lost. Time passed rapidly, as quickly as the sky grew black. I eventually regained the road, soaked to the skin.' Here Robin paused and fell silent. I began to wonder whether he was having second thoughts about finishing his story.

'Now, you've got to believe what I'm going to tell you!' I noticed that his glass of beer had remained untouched for several minutes.

'There I was on the edge of one of the busiest roads in England, with cars and lorries thundering past me, throwing up great walls of spray. I was dripping wet and beginning to feel very cold. And Milford was but a few minutes drive down the road. You know I don't like cars but I swallowed my pride and decided to try to hitch a lift. I stood by the roadside near where the lane goes down to Waggoners Wells, thumbing as hard as I could. But would any of them stop! Like heck! I admit that by this time I must have looked a rather strange sight. Once or twice cars did seem to slow down a bit only to accelerate away again as soon as they saw me clearly. Can't blame them really, I suppose. So, bedraggled and bowed, I began to trudge my soggy way towards Hindhead, still raising my thumb occasionally in the hope that someone would take pity on me. The traffic was almost continuous now but no one stopped.'

'I was almost up to the bend, dodging between the trees not far from the Spaniard Inn. Very slowly, it seemed, I became aware that something had changed. A peace, a tranquillity had descended upon the road. Then I realised why — all the traffic had gone — the road was completely empty. Only the patter of the heavy rain reached my ears. There was not even the song of an optimistic thrush to break the strange silence. Although not quite official twilight, the dark clouds made it very murky. I looked back down the road, hoping to see the lights of approaching vehicles, but there were none. I had a distinct feeling of unease. I couldn't explain why at the time. I told myself not to be stupid.'

'Then I saw the lights coming towards me up the hill. They were very dim at first and moving silently it seemed. As the vehicle drew nearer I could see the outline of a sleek, black saloon of the 1930s period, a large Vauxhall or even a Buick, perhaps. When it was almost upon me, without thinking, I raised my thumb. For a moment the driver appeared to ignore me just like all the rest, but a few yards beyond me the car came to a stop. I hesitated a second or two but, despite my feeling of unease, I ran towards the car. Might as well get to Milford in style, I comforted myself. The nearside door was locked so I walked round the vehicle and got in on the offside, sitting myself down behind the driver, profusely thanking him for stopping.'

'There were, I think, three men in the car but none of them said a word of greeting or even acknowledged my existence. The backs of the heads of the driver and his front seat passenger gradually became clear as my eyes adjusted themselves to the gloom inside. They sat looking straight ahead, and neither turned to view their new passenger. My companion in the back seat was equally uncommunicative. His head was turned away from me and he seemed totally preoccupied with the view from his window. The car moved quietly off. Good, I thought, I'll be home in a quarter of an hour.'

' "Horrible weather now isn't it, considering what a nice morning it was?" I said to my silent fellow travellers. But there was still no response as the car sped rapidly up the hill towards the traffic lights at the Hindhead crossroads. The towards the traffic lights at the Hindhead crossroads. The men sat motionless. I now became aware of a nasty, musty, damp smell in the car. It was so overpowering that it quickly made me feel rather sick. The seat felt damp and so very cold. I very much looked forward to getting out at Milford. "Could you drop me off at Milford, please, thanks very much," I said. Still no response. I could see the green light at the crossroads in the distance. I began to feel concerned. Were these men deaf? How could I get them to stop at Milford, I wondered?'

'When the car was about fifty yards from the lights, they turned to red. Perhaps I should exit here, to be safe, I thought. I felt for the door handle. I couldn't find it and the inside of the door was slimy to the touch. Then I noticed that the window on my side appeared to be covered in green algae. The car sped on, showing no sign of slowing for the lights. When he does stop I'll definitely jump out, I told myself. In the dark I found something which I thought was the door handle but when I tried a test pull on it, it came away in my hands.'

'The red light was now upon us. I could see cars beginning to cross from the Haslemere direction. If the driver didn't stop there would be a crash. But then the weirdest thing happened — we sped over the crossroads as if we or the other cars weren't there. I closed my eyes and waited for the crunch, but nothing happened. I was terrified. "Let me out, now," I shouted at the top of my voice! Then the front seat passenger craned his head round, very slowly, to look at me. I swear I shall remember that look until I die. It was a look from beyond the grave. His eyes glowed with a phosphorescence difficult to describe — piercing, turning my heart to ice. But while his eyes burned, his face was that of a corpse. His pale, dessicated lips were drawn back as if in agony and his teeth gleamed white in the now disappearing lights of Hindhead.'

'In panic I frantically banged my shoulder against the door. Even falling out of the car at some speed was preferable to that stare. And now the man sitting next to me also turned his head in my direction. I fancy I heard his neck bones click. His face was horribly mutilated — his jaw hung loose and his skin was shredded and then there were his eyes. They seemed almost to mock me as they glowed white in the dark.'

'The car was now going down the steep hill, approaching that notoriously sharp left-hand bend above the Devil's Punchbowl. It was going much too fast. I had to get out before I became a victim of yet another fatal car crash upon that spot. I pushed at the door with all my force. The eyes, the eyes, they would not go away. We were almost at the bend now. There was a squeal of tyres as the car tried to make it round the corner. I pushed and banged. Eventually the door gave way just as the car left the road to plummet down into the dark depths of the Punchbowl. I must have fallen out but I can't really recall what happened next. I do remember feeling a searing pain in my leg, of seeing the eyes, those terrible eyes and then — nothing.'

'Well, John, the rest of the story you know already. They were a lovely couple who found me. They came to see me in hospital but my words failed to show the level of my gratitude to them.'

We sat in silence in that cosy pub, both lost in our thoughts for a long time.

'You have to believe me, John,' he implored. 'You're the first person I've told. I should have let you into the secret long ago. I can still see those eyes, you know. I can never forget them!'

'I believe you, Robin, although I'm sure many wouldn't. Now, drink up your pint. Did you find any interesting old bottles, by the way?'

10

The Mystery
of Haroldslea

THE sound was faint at first but unmistakable. Floating over the fields on the mists and vapours of an autumn evening, tolling cold fear in the peaceful family sheltering in their home before the blazing fire. The old sheepdog had felt it before they heard it. His hackles rose and, yellow toothed, he snarled and then stopped, listened again and growled long and low. The family gathered closer to the fire for protection, but shivered cold and clammy when they heard it too.

It was like this every year on this one particular day in November. A bell, deep and sonorous, tolled slow doom, still faint while the sun even now hovered above the horizon. The people hid in the attic or the cellar, trying to block the sound from their minds but there was no respite from its eerie clang. Wherever they went it was there, growing louder now as the sun finally plunged from sight, its golden afterglow touching hedgerow and tree, house and barn.

The house in question was Haroldslea near Horley, built in the 18th century on a site with a long history. This place probably originated as a simple dwelling in an area in the forest cleared by a Saxon named Herewald. In medieval times it was owned by the Countess de Warrenne and later by Reginald de Cobham. Behind Haroldslea House was an orchard and, down among the trees, an ancient well, now disused, deep and dark, with a bottom which could not be seen, even in bright daylight. A stone would drop silently down for an age before there came back a faint splash.

Nearby, the claggy remains of Thunderfield Castle have their history too. The name dates back to pagan Saxon times when the people worshipped many gods, including Thor, the God of Thunder and 'defender of the world'. His name, if not his memory still survives — the fifth day of the week is the 'day of thunder', Thursday. In the reign of King Stephen, days of lawlessness and anarchy, Thunderfield was fortified by the de Clares of Bletchingley. All that remains now is a damp and stinking moat, a sombre place where the air is chill and the tolling of a bell has sometimes been heard.

It was the sound of that same bell which froze the hearts of those at Haroldslea. As darkness came on so did that solemn tone. Slowly ever nearer it crept, across clammy meadows and fields, through autumn woods of russet leaves and the damp smell of decay. Louder and louder it came. Now, as midnight approached, it was in the orchard, its eerie tolling and mingling echo could be heard in the depths of the well. Then the sound slowly faded and was gone.

Every year the tolling bell was expected on that day, 11th November, and every year it was heard, not only by the people at Haroldslea House but by many a villager as well.

But one year, it was 1938, there was silence. As the sun rolled orange red to the lip of the land, the family waited ready, tense and nervous, pretending to be acting normally, reading or sewing, with only the tick of the clock breaking the quiet still coming of the night. Gradually a chill mist floated from field and wood towards the house.

It was a dark, black night that came quite suddenly and the silence was like death. Nothing moved inside or out. Apprehension hung motionless in the air. The dog slept before the muted fire, scarcely breathing. The tingling senses became unbearable. The book was laid to one side and the dexterous fingers stilled.

Again, it was the dog who sensed it first, head instantly lifted, eyes wide, teeth drawn together growling, then a terrified howl followed by a soft whimper. The people heard the bell then, almost with relief. But, as it came closer, there was another noise, rhythmic and deep. What was it? Closer, gradually closer, the tolling bell and . . . , there was no mistaking it, the sound of tramping feet, the sound of an army on the march.

On, on they came, closer and closer. Now they were marching through the orchard and up the garden path, heading towards the house. The people stood up, expecting someone or something to knock at the stout oak door, but still these unseen troops marched on, the grating thud of their boots echoing into every room.

Suddenly, through the unopened door they appeared, marching two by two, grey-helmeted heads pushed forward, chain mail glinting in the lamplight, eyes straight ahead, staring purposefully towards their hidden goal. Strangely these fighting men carried no weapons — marching, marching, on and on. The people covered their ears, standing stock still with the shock of it all. More and more soldiers followed, tramping right through the house from the orchard at the back to the roadway at the front, solid brick and wood no barrier to their progress. But eventually there were no more.

When they had gone, and the sound of their marching had become an echo in the mind, the people sank back in their chairs, shocked and numb. The air in the house was icy cold despite that blazing fire. The silence which followed was not peaceful but full of foreboding.

Then they heard it again — the bell tolling slow and clear from deep in the well in the orchard. But gradually the sound subsided, fading away in the darkness. It was midnight and another year had passed.

11

The Haunting of Wotton House

WOTTON House, near Dorking, is chiefly known as the birthplace in 1620 of the diarist and horticulturist, John Evelyn. But Evelyn would have difficulty in recognising the house he knew so well if he returned today, because of extensive alterations and additions made during the centuries since his death in 1706. However, he would undoubtedly still feel at home in the house's impressive garden, much of which he designed during the middle years of the 17th century.

Wotton has a long history as the seat of the Evelyn family and the core of the house dates from Tudor times. The shadows of history stalk every room and corridor, recalling the lives and deaths of the many generations who have lived within its walls. It is not surprising that, from time to time, there comes evidence of the return of those who found fun or tragedy here in the years before our time.

More recently the house has ceased to be a family home

and has had a variety of other uses. Until the early 1980s it was the Fire Service Staff College and during the day its corridors echoed to thump and clatter of well-polished boots and shoes. Many firemen have fond memories of studying here and some of these cool, calm and level-headed men can also tell of weird, inexplicable occurrences. Various small objects would disappear and then turn up again in unusual places, and sash windows would open of their own accord. Then there were those cold places where not even the heat of a summer day could remove the chill, or the strange, anxious atmosphere. But it was those men who guarded Wotton House by night who had the most tales to tell.

Night porter, Mr Welch, was on duty through the dark hours of 2nd April 1964. It was a bitterly cold night, and manning the reception desk was not one of the most comfortable of duties. On that quiet, still night perhaps he dozed fitfully, but then he heard the front door open gently and softly close. The figure of a man then appeared from near the door and walked silently across the hall towards a table on the left-hand side of the hall fireplace. It was a most unusual looking visitor indeed.

'He was very short — say four feet or less,' reported Mr Welch. 'He was wearing a hairy brown tweed jacket and dark trousers, and was carrying something long under his left arm.'

The 'something' under this nocturnal dwarf's arm was oddly indistinct. 'But I knew it to be fishing tackle,' said the night porter. 'He had very little white or grey hair and long Dickensian whiskers — rather sparse, white, and swept out sideways.'

The figure paused by the table. 'To look at something on the table, or so it seemed. I had the impression of tranquillity and a kindly face.' It seemed as if the lower part of his legs were indistinct or missing. As he paused by the table Mr Welch asked him politely if he could be of any help. 'He did not answer, and never gave any sign that he knew I was there. He never looked in my direction.'

The figure seemed unhurried but a trifle fussily pre-occupied. After a moment or two spent by the table he moved towards the door and then 'he just wasn't there anymore'. Mr Welch looked at his watch. It was just five minutes to three.

It was the feeling of tranquillity and that kindly face which left the most lasting impression on the Wotton House night porter. 'I did not have the "cold" sensation and was not in the least alarmed,' he emphasized.

Who was this piscatorial visitor and why was he so small? There are no records of any men of such stature living in the house. William John Evelyn, whose life at Wotton spanned part of the last century and this, had a reputation for keeping exotic pets, but not of the human species. The ruins of his 'Turtle or Tortoise House' stand among the undergrowth near the house. He was responsible for the introduction of kangaroos to the Surrey fauna when some of his collection of antipodean marsupials escaped. They lived and bred for many years on the surrounds of Leith Hill nearby and gave many an unsuspecting hiker a shock of ghostly proportions.

The explanation for the diminutive stature of the ghost seen by Mr Welch may be found in the development over the centuries of the building itself. In a house continually added to and altered, it is possible that the figure was not as short as it appeared. The ghost of a man of normal height may walk upon the floor of his time, a floor now buried deep below the present. Thus he will appear, in that fleeting glimpse of past and present superimposed, to be well under his proper height.

Mr Welch was not the only porter to witness the arrival of such uninvited guests during his night-time vigil. Although his ghost was not of the frightening kind, other apparitions, less friendly, also stalked the corridors and rooms of Wotton House.

One night a porter at reception was expecting the late return of a member of staff. It was a clear night and the cloudless sky was full of ice cold points of light. A strong wind blew, whining through the bare trees, whipping up the last of the autumn leaves and dropping them mischievously upon the well-kept gravel drive. Suddenly the wind stopped dead and the air was still. The cold draught which had long been gnawing at the man's feet, now seemed to freeze around him. And then he heard the footsteps crunching and grinding upon the gravel, making their way towards the front door. Thinking it was the member of staff, the porter went to the door and opened it to offer greetings. The footsteps ceased. There was no one there. Then, just as suddenly as it had ceased, the wind got up again and something unseen pushed past him into the hall. Mystified, the man paused in the half open doorway until the chill nudged him back into the present, and then he shut the door hard.

He went back to the reception desk and for a while the night returned to normal. The man gave up his questions to rational conclusions as the wind rose even stronger than before. Small clouds began to move across the sky, switching off the stars along their course. There might be rain before the light of day. And then the wind dropped again, and in the stillness came those footsteps once more, walking firmly towards the door. This time the porter stayed put at his desk in a muddle of indecision. The front door opened, the man looked up.

What he saw was there and then not. At times he could see right through it, hazy and grey — the shape of a man, a shadow walking slowly now without a sound. It did not hesitate but moved with purpose across the hall and along the corridor. The man got up and began to follow but as his courage grew the image faded. When he had walked a little way he realised with some annoyance that it was gone.

Perhaps the figure was making its way towards the oak-panelled room on the first floor, which was sometimes used as a bedroom for guests and visiting lecturers. Some refused to sleep there after the first night, complaining of the cold and the intimidating atmosphere. This room had its secrets and some who emerged, pale and drawn after a sleepless night, were not prepared to say exactly why. The only access to the room was via an antechamber. This room was the exact opposite to its neighbour - it was cosy and comforting and here the night porters often took a break to brew a cup of tea.

One night a group of them were doing just that — a good cupper can do wonders to relieve the monotony of an uneventful night. Uneventful that is until, during a lull in the conversation, they heard the unmistakable sound of creaking floorboards in the panelled room next door. But the room was unoccupied and the door from the antechamber firmly locked. Whatever was making the sound progressed slowly towards the door. This the men sensed rather than heard, sensed the growing evil within the room beyond. Conversation froze as all eyes looked towards the door. Perhaps they should just get up and unlock it, for there ought to be a logical explanation. But, although not a word was said, the same thoughts were in every mind and there they sat, waiting.

Only the thickness of the door now separated the men from something of menace within the panelled room. Then the door handle creaked and began to move downwards very slowly. With no thought of joking banter to break the silence, their eyes were transfixed by that moving handle as it returned, almost imperceptibly, to its former position. It began to move down again, but this time a little more quickly and back again. Dank fear began to invade the watchers as their tea grew cold. Gradually the movement of the door handle became faster. Faster and faster, now frantically, it rattled up and down. The door seemed almost to bulge towards them under the pressure from within, but it and the lock held firm. After what seemed an age the movement slowed, the pressure lessened, and then it stopped.

The Wotton porters sat for a long time in numbed silence, not taking their eyes from that door, not sure if the evil had passed. Eventually, one of them took a deep breath, got up stiffly from his chair, and stood before the door. He waited awhile before slowly and as quietly as he could, he turned the key. Grasping the handle, he suddenly shoved the door open. It swung back violently, releasing the icy air trapped within.

They hesitated to proceed beyond the threshold. Perhaps they would after another cup of tea, they thought. But finally curiosity brought sufficient courage. The light switch was reached with difficulty. When they finally entered it was, as they had always known, just an empty room.

12

Mirror, Mirror . . .

'THIS towne hath very fair inns and good entertainment at the tavernes, the Angell, the Crowne, the White Hart and the Lyon,' wrote the poet, John Taylor, in 1636. Confirmation, indeed, that the many travellers passing through Guildford could be sure of a comfortable haven even then. Through the 18th and 19th centuries this ancient town's inns prospered. But decline began when the railway came and only the Angel survives, leaving us a mere trace of High Street life before the motorcar.

The Angel itself was threatened, shuttered and closed for many months, the speed of modern transport seeming literally to have overtaken it. Fortunately its door has reopened. Now light and dark mix once more along its historic corridors and through its comfortable bedrooms. And in some of those rooms come whispers from the past, a hint of a presence felt only by a few, a chill there awhile and gone, imagination for real.

Sitting in the lounge I have felt it and up on the landing, where I crept to have a look for what I thought would be the last time. But in the so-called crypt restaurant in the basement there was nothing but a medieval shop, happy in prosperity, where maybe only claustrophobia makes the mind play tricks. Here I purloined a copy of the last menu for the archives and made a hasty exit.

A number of visitors to the Angel over the years have reported strange happenings in various parts of the building. Not necessarily striking fear but rather curiosity, and perhaps this is how it sometimes should be.

In January 1970, Mr and Mrs Dell from Bayswater stayed for a weekend at the Angel. They were given Room One, the Prince Imperial of France Room, on the first floor overlooking the High Street, named with obvious clarity after an earlier resident. This bedroom did not have a reputation for being haunted. However, two months before, there had been a curious incident involving a woman who had booked into the room.

At about eight o'clock that evening the receptionist on the hotel switchboard answered a call from the Room One extension but no one spoke. The switchboard light stayed on but still there was silence, so the receptionist went upstairs to investigate. She found the woman standing in the middle of the bedroom rooted to the spot with fear. Although she found it difficult to explain, the woman claimed that she was acutely aware of a presence and asked to be moved to another room. Room One was regularly occupied during the following weeks but the incident was not repeated. By the time the Dells booked in, most of the staff had forgotten about it completely.

The Prince Imperial of France Room was comfortably furnished. One significant piece of furniture in the heavily beamed double room was a massive wardrobe with a seven foot by four foot mirror as its centre piece. After an

75

excellent meal in the restaurant below, the Dells retired for what they hoped would be a good night's sleep.

A strange bed can sometimes take a night or two to get used to, as Mr Dell found out. When he awoke yet again it was nearly 3 o'clock in the morning. He got out of bed and went and sat in one of the armchairs, half turned towards the wardrobe. All the room seemed quiet and peaceful. There were no strange noises and Mr Dell felt no chill as he sat for just a few minutes before returning to bed.

When he finally got up out of the armchair he glanced casually at the wardrobe mirror as he did so, and promptly fell back into the chair. He was not sure whether to be frightened or perplexed. He sat transfixed for several moments staring hard. He must be wrong. Was he still asleep? In the mirror he could clearly see the reflection of a man. But when he looked in the direction where the man should be there was nothing.

The figure was visible only from the waist up. A middle aged man with a large dark moustache, dressed in what appeared to be some form of military uniform. Mr Dell sat fascinated, unsure what to do next. He whispered to his wife, who woke up, got out of bed and came and joined him near the mirror. At first Mrs Dell could not see what her husband was talking about but gradually, as her eyes became accustomed to the light from the street outside, she saw it too. It was quite plainly there, but when she turned away from the mirror the room looked perfectly normal and undisturbed.

The man did not move at all, not even his eyes. His face bore a compelling expression, dark eyes under heavy eyebrows, staring into the mirror. Mr Dell had the presence of mind to reach for a red serviette, the only paper handy, and his blue ball-point pen. Carefully and slowly he began to make a sketch of what they both could see. The figure remained unflinching, a perfect model, while Mr Dell finished his drawing. The uniform looked foreign he thought. The drawing finished to the best of his ability, the couple sat motionless until the man just faded away. Mr Dell noted that the image must have been visible for about half an hour.

The following evening after dinner he told the manager, Mr Kiersz, what he and his wife had clearly seen the night before. He was adamant that it was a ghost, saying he was willing to testify as to the truth of what they said.

If the Prince Imperial of France room was haunted, who by? The story was soon reported by the *Surrey Advertiser*, who reproduced Mr Dell's nocturnal drawing with the article. The man, looking very much like a soldier, certainly appeared anything but British. But who can tell? Nothing in history pointed to a solution and no one came forward with a single clue to solve the mystery. It is now over twenty years since the sighting and no other guest staying in Room One has seen the man. So a mystery it must remain but, one night, someone may awake from peaceful slumber to find the answer in the mirror.

13

The Prisoner

THE woman sat comfortably in the bedroom armchair. She gently closed her eyes, her hands resting upon her lap, finger tips lightly pressed together. There was a long silence. The woman seemed to fall asleep, breathing deeply and rhythmically, as she drifted into a trance. All was quiet and peaceful within the house. Outside, only the faintest of breezes whispered through the tops of the gnarled old trees that cast grey shadows upon the house. The leaves rustled words that few could hear and even fewer understand.

Suddenly the woman underwent a remarkable change. Her breathing quickened. Her body became rigid and stretched out in the chair. Her lips contorted and quivered, trying to speak the words of another entity which now possessed her. But no intelligible words passed her struggling lips. She gasped and gurgled and fought for air. Then she let out an eerie moaning marked with the pain and anguish of a past which made peace beyond the grave impossible.

The watchers gathered in the bedroom shuddered silently, their eyes fixed unflinchingly upon the woman. They had come to Ash Manor to discover the strange secrets of its haunting. Now the restless spirit was trying to reach them through the woman who struggled before them.

Ash Manor is a rambling half-timbered house, just a mile or two from the Hampshire border, with a history going back to the 14th century. It is still partly surrounded by a moat, while inside there are heavy oak beams and a large inglenook fireplace.

Mr and Mrs Kelly and their sixteen year old daughter, Patricia, came to live in the old house in 1934. Mr Kelly was a member of the family who had become a household name thanks to the many directories they had published since the 1840s. In the tranquil surroundings of the house, situated well back from any road amidst 24 acres, they hoped to find contentment. But the Kellys seemed to be a family particularly susceptible to psychic phenomena and at Ash Manor they would find no peace.

It was late evening just a few short weeks after the family had moved in. Mr Kelly and his daughter had already gone to bed. Mrs Kelly still bustled about the house, attending to a few odd matters before she too went upstairs. There was the occasional noise as the house settled down in the cool of the night — almost imperceptible creaks and clicks but nothing out of the ordinary. Outside the night was quiet with just a little wind to push the occasional cloud across a starry sky.

As Mrs Kelly began to climb the Jacobean staircase something made her stop — a noise, almost nothing, the faint moaning of the wind in the trees, perhaps. But then it became louder and now she could distinctly hear groaning.

She shuddered at the sound. Someone was in pain, great pain, and their suffering writhed through the house. Thinking it might be her husband, she rushed up the remaining stairs but found Mr Kelly already sound asleep. He must have been dreaming, she considered logically. Hearing nothing more, she resolved to ask him about his dreams at breakfast next morning. Soon she too was asleep. Outside, the trees stood like dark sentinels, guarding the secrets of the ancient house, witnesses to the long years of anguish within its walls.

Next morning brought no solution as to the source of the horrifying sounds Mrs Kelly had heard. Her husband told her of a restful night with no dreams which remained within his memory. Her daughter had heard nothing. Mrs Kelly knew she had not imagined the terrible groaning of the night before, but she was sure they must have come from her husband. Unless . . .

A few nights later, when all three were sitting chatting or reading in the lounge, its low ceiling heavy with dark beams, they all heard something that they knew could not be explained. Footsteps — something walking slowly along the upstairs corridor in a house whose three living occupants were all downstairs. Walking back and forth with faltering step. Was it coming down the stairs? Much to their relief it was not, but it continued its hesitant progress above their heads for quite some time. Then the sound faded and was gone.

The Kellys heard the footsteps on many occasions after that but no stranger was ever seen walking that upstairs corridor. However, early one evening, when Mr Kelly was in his bedroom, the figure of a man appeared, standing by the window. The man was oddly dressed but looked so lifelike that he thought it was an intruder. He flung himself upon the figure but ended up clutching at thin air and, losing his balance, he slipped upon the polished floor and fell heavily.

The footsteps came regularly as the months passed into years. Their faltering presence was heard about the deserted passages, up and down, up and down, sounding like the steps of a tortured prisoner. And with it came the incessant groans, forcing the family to share their unwanted companion's many agonies. The Kellys tried to make light of it and they succeeded for quite some time but, when Mr Kelly saw the apparition at the window once more, the family realised they needed help. And so, one day in July 1937, a party of psychic researchers arrived at Ash Manor to try to find the cause of the haunting. They included an American medium, Mrs Garrett, and from her lips came the ghost's first attempts to tell of a troubled past.

For fully fifteen minutes the spirit struggled. The woman gasped and moaned but some physical impediment seemed to block the way to speech. Eventually some of the watchers lifted the woman's head for fear that she was choking. She slowly raised one hand and pointed to her lips. Her mouth fell open, her tongue lolled uselessly between her teeth. Her hand made further signs which they eventually understood. This spirit had no tongue. It had been mutilated whilst he lived. The woman rose up from the chair and fell upon her knees and a single word broke from her lips, 'Eleison'. Was this the troubled spirit's name? But was it not Greek? 'Kyrie, eleison' — 'Lord, have mercy', the spirit begged his persecutors.

Very gradually speech seemed to come more easily and slowly part of the confused story was told. During a period of civil strife, perhaps in late medieval times, his wife had been taken by the enemy and his son killed in battle. He was imprisoned in Ash Manor and held in chains for over thirty years. During that time he was starved and tortured and, when his groans unnerved his gaolers, they slit his tongue to keep him quiet. And so his spirit lingered on in the house after death, seeking vengeance for the horror of his life.

After several further seances the tortured spirit was persuaded to rid himself of those destructive thoughts of vengeance, and to go to his lost wife and son. Now the psychic researchers felt they had succeeded in ridding Ash Manor of its ghostly suffering. Indeed, it is supposedly true that the groans and faltering steps were heard no more. But possibly the suffering was in some way too ingrained in the place and an unhappy presence continued to haunt Ash Manor.

Tragedy, like the shadows of the trees now gone still fell upon the house. We shall never know if Mr Kelly ever saw the apparition in the bedroom again or heard that terrible sound of pain. In April 1950 he was consumed by his own suffering. An electricity inspector calling at the house found him lying on the front lawn. Two letters and a bottle of cyanide of potassium were found near him. Maurice Kelly was dead.

14

The Moodiwarp

M Y name is David McLellan. You ask me if I believe in ghosts and I think I do. Many years ago when I was about ten I had a dream but perhaps it wasn't a dream, I'm still not sure. It was certainly a frightening experience, no doubt about it. This is my story. You can come to your own conclusions.

'I think we'll run down to Reigate to see Marjorie,' said my mother one bright spring morning in early May.

I greeted the idea with great enthusiasm. Reigate was a town of great mystery to me as a boy in the early 1950s. It is hard to believe that now when, like most of Surrey's ancient towns, it has been brought down to earth, so to speak, by the ceaseless roar of modern traffic. Now the drivers of cars and vans, with the accelerator full on the aggression, speed round its one-way racetrack. But thirty-five years ago things were different. Its ancient buildings breathed in another world and the brick arches of the old town hall hid a hundred ghosts of Reigate's past in their shadowy corners. To me the town had an atmosphere which was far removed from the suburbia of Sutton where we lived.

In those days what heightened the young imagination with dreams of Ruritania was the manner of our entrance into the town. The car rolled down Reigate Hill from the chalk scarp of the North Downs, bumped over the railway level crossing, went on a little further and, with a large hill looming in front of us, we promptly disappeared into a long, dark tunnel. Here was mystery indeed. Amidst the echoing clatter and thump of an engine past its prime, we suddenly emerged, without warning, into the bright light of day and the very centre of Reigate. If we had known then of Doctor Who, we would surely have likened the experience to going through a time warp!

Marjorie lived over a shop. I seem to remember that it was a hairdresser's. Her living room overlooked the street and was often filled with smells which varied between sweet perfume and bad eggs. Marjorie was a dark-haired lady with impenetrable grey eyes and she came from Yorkshire. She was very tall. I remember when I first met her that she seemed to have a permanent stoop. But when we went shopping one day she towered above me and I realised that it was only the low ceilings of her home which made her bend.

That day in May we arrived at her home in time for lunch, with the prospect afterwards of exploring the humps and lumps and the mock gatehouse, which are all that is left of Reigate Castle. But, unseen, as we tucked into the excellent food that Marjorie always provided, grey clouds rolled up. They began to deposit much of their contents on Reigate just at the time when we had intended to go out.

Marjorie lived alone. I think her husband had been killed in the war and her son, Norman, was married and lived in Gosport. Fortunately for me he had left behind his Dinky toys so I was never disappointed when it rained. And

rain it certainly did that afternoon. You could hear it
pounding on the roof and gurgling down the gutter pipe.
Outside, there came that shushing sound as the occasional
car splashed past through the ever-growing puddles.

It was about seven o'clock in the evening when, after an
excellent tea, my mother decided we must go. The rain had
eased off a little as we climbed into the car with goodbyes
said and promises of an early return. The starter motor
cranked, and cranked again but the engine refused to fire.
Mother tried yet again but still with no success — the
ignition was dead, perhaps drowned by the Reigate rain. It
was too late for the local garage and the emergency service
might be a bit expensive.

Marjorie was soon suggesting that we should stay the
night. Norman was coming up next morning and he was a
genius with all things mechanical. After a quick phone call
home everything was settled. Mother would have
Norman's old room and I would sleep in the tiny box room
at the back.

'You'll be all right in there,' said Marjorie, but with a little
hesitation.

After a supper of more of Marjorie's Dundee cake, I was
hustled off to bed. My bedroom was a strange, tiny room. It
had a ceiling which sloped right down almost to the small
bed against one wall. There was a pile of boxes in one
corner and a small chest of drawers along the opposite wall.
There was just about enough room to squeeze between the
drawers and the bed. The floor was covered with murky
brown, cold lino. Although Marjorie had given the room a
quick clean before I went to bed, the light which hung from
the apex of the ceiling was festooned with black cobwebs.
Lying in bed waiting for the 'goodnights' from the adults, I
could see the cobwebs sagging in the dark recesses of the

room, like rope bridges in the Andes. There was one small window, now covered with some oppressive looking faded maroon curtains.

Eventually the light was switched off and, with the door left ajar for my confidence, I soon drifted into a deep and dreamless sleep. But was it dreamless? Was what happened that night but a dream, a product of my fertile imagination? Whatever it was it was real enough to me.

At some point in the night I gradually found myself awake. I was strangely hot and the air in that tiny room was stifling. As my eyes became accustomed to my surroundings I was alarmed to see that the bedroom door was shut, or almost shut. My jacket hung from a peg behind the door. I stared at it for a long time and then it seemed to take on life. I swear I saw it move. In clammy fear I dived beneath the bedclothes and lay paralysed. How long I stayed like that I cannot say, but eventually I had to come up for air. I turned over very slowly onto my stomach so I could not see the door.

The silence at that moment was dense and tangible. But it was suddenly penetrated by a scratching noise, like a dog trying to get in. Now I could feel my heart racing and hear the thump of my pulse in my ears. But Marjorie has no pets. I tried to cry out but my mouth was gagged with a rasping dryness, and my shout came out as a feeble croak.

I'm sure I heard the door swing slowly open, letting in a draught of icy air. The scratching was now in the room — something scratching and snuffling. Now it climbed onto the bed — I could not look. I could feel something rubbing against the backs of my legs and feel the weight of it moving at the end of the bed. Only the thinness of a blanket and sheet separated me from its touch. Its movements were slightly jerky and I fancied I could feel its claws. The beating in my ears was reaching a crescendo — my head would surely burst.

But, just as it had come, it went. The weight came off the bed and quickly all was quiet and still. I lay in clammy fear for an age before I summoned up my courage and turned over. I opened my eyes. The bedroom door was slightly ajar and my jacket hung limp and motionless from the peg.

I must have fallen asleep again for the next thing I remember was hearing the curtains being drawn back. I opened my eyes, the light streamed in.

'I've brought you a nice cup of tea,' said Marjorie. 'Sleep well?' she enquired.

'I don't know,' I said slowly, as the memories of the night quickly flooded back. 'I think I had a nasty dream.' Marjorie squeezed back past the chest of drawers and sat down on the end of the bed. 'What sort of dream?' she asked.

I then told her of the events of the night. 'It seemed so real. I'm sure it couldn't have been a dream,' I emphasized.

'Funny you should say that,' said Marjorie. 'A few years ago a friend of Norman's stayed in this room but he ended up sleeping on the settee in the living room. He had almost exactly the same experience — sorry, dream, as you,' she continued. 'But he claimed to have seen what it was. . . . Oh! I shouldn't be telling you this or you'll never want to stay here again.'

'Go on, please!'

'Well, what he said he saw at the end of the bed was at first dark and almost shapeless. But then it developed into some sort of animal with a pointed nose and he was sure he could see a pair of beady little eyes staring menacingly at him. I said to him that it sounded like a mole, but he was sure it was much bigger than that. It was difficult to tell as its form appeared to keep on changing as it moved about the foot of the bed. Finally it just faded away. We joked about it afterwards. We called it the moodiwarp.'

'What's that mean?' I asked, finding the sound of the name a little disturbing.

'Well, it's an old Yorkshire word for a mole,' Marjorie replied. 'Yes, moodiwarp, that's what we called it,' she mumbled almost to herself.

Later that morning Norman and his family arrived. In what seemed like no time at all, our car was running sweetly.

'You'll know how to do that one day,' said Norman cheerfully to me.

By lunchtime we were back in Sutton and the incidents of the night were pushed to the back of my mind, but never quite forgotten.

Over the next year or two we made the occasional trip to Reigate to see Marjorie, but we never stayed overnight again. Then Marjorie remarried and she and her new husband emigrated to New Zealand. The families kept in touch for a few years and then the link was broken. I sometimes wonder if the moodiwarp went with her. But perhaps someone in Reigate knows otherwise.

15

Soapy Sam

I DOUBT if there have been many leading men of the Church who have claimed to have seen a ghost, but Bishop Samuel Wilberforce was at least one. He was the son of William Wilberforce, who successfully fought for the abolition of slavery. From an early age Wilberforce junior was destined for a career in the Church. He was an excellent preacher and 'a very quick, lively, and agreeable man'. In 1845, within fifteen years of being ordained, he was enthroned as Bishop of Oxford. In 1869 he became the Bishop of Winchester.

Surrey has no shortage of ghostly monks but we should, perhaps, be wary of the authenticity of most of them. However, when the source is one of the leading churchmen of the last century, who can deny this particular apparition its place in history.

It was during the early 1840s, when Wilberforce was a canon of Winchester, that he visited a Roman Catholic family in Surrey. Unfortunately, he did not record exactly where this family lived, wishing, no doubt, to preserve their anonymity. One evening, as he came down to dinner, he passed a silent hooded figure on the stairs. He thought it looked like a monk, but one which appeared to be very much flesh and blood. At dinner Wilberforce enquired about the monk. Without any element of surprise his hosts described the family ghost. The apparition wandered the rooms of the house searching for something, they knew not what. They claimed that the monk had died in tragic circumstances, leaving his work unfinished and his troubled spirit to walk the rooms and corridors of their ancient home. They had no fear of him.

Wilberforce was a prolific author and researcher and was particularly keen to study certain works in his guests' library. The family had amassed an excellent collection of books, some quite rare. Therefore, late that evening, when most of the family had gone to bed, he went into the library. He was sitting reading, his notebook at hand, when, quite suddenly and without the opening of the door, the monk was there in front of him, searching along the bookcases, looking this way and that. The apparition's features were clearly visible to Wilberforce. When the monk stopped at a particular bay of books those features took on a perplexed then agitated look.

At this point Wilberforce asked the monk calmly and firmly if he could be of any assistance. Not expecting any reply, he was most surprised when the apparition, who the family had said was silent, began to speak. Wilberforce found it hard to believe that he was having a conversation with someone from beyond the grave. When the monk spoke his words were clear and normal. This was no sombre voice of ghostly echoes, just a voice heavy with concern. He told Wilberforce that hidden above the bookcase there was a sheaf of papers which contained information harmful to the family. The papers must be destroyed. But this could only be done successfully by someone outside their circle. The monk had chosen a 'receptive' person to carry out this imperative task.

Wilberforce moved the library steps over to the bookcase indicated by the monk. He climbed slowly and deliberately to the highest step and stretched up to peer over the top. For a moment he saw nothing amongst the dust and cobwebs, but then he spotted a tightly rolled bundle jammed into a tiny recess behind the carved frieze. He brought the papers carefully down amidst clouds of dust. He must not look at them the monk insisted, no one must see them again.

The fire in the library grate was almost dead, but the last few embers still glowed faintly orange. Without another thought Wilberforce tossed the grimy bundle onto those last few coals. For an age he watched as the papers slowly curled. The monk watched too. Then faint wisps of smoke came from beneath and small flames began licking at the edges. Suddenly the fire gained a hold and soon those incriminating papers were but a ball of flame, then dark thin ashes.

Wilberforce sat watching the fire to the end, feeling at peace. Perhaps the monk felt so too. Wilberforce turned to face his companion but the man had gone. The monk was never seen again.

At one point in his career Samuel Wilberforce gained an unfair reputation for being rather evasive. In 1864 one of his synodical judgements was described by Lord Westbury as 'a well-lubricated set of words, a sentence so oily and saponaceous that no one can grasp it'. Wilberforce's characteristic reply to that was that 'though often in hot water, he always came out with clean hands'. These exchanges led to Wilberforce acquiring the nickname 'Soapy Sam'.

It is curious that, having reported a ghostly experience in his lifetime, Soapy Sam should become in death a ghost himself. When he became Bishop of Winchester in 1869 his new diocese included a very large part of Surrey. This area is now the bulk of the Diocese of Guildford which was created in 1927. One day in 1873 he was riding with Lord Granville to the latter's house at Holmbury St Mary. As they rode through Deerleap Wood only a short distance north of Wotton House, the bishop remarked that he had never found the time to visit the Evelyn family home. Having written a biography of Mrs Godolphin many years before, he had always been keen to go to Wotton to see a painting of the lady which hung there.

It was just a few moments later that the accident happened. Riding at a swift canter, Wilberforce's horse suddenly slipped and stumbled. The unfortunate bishop was ejected from the saddle and took a crashing fall. Looking back, Lord Granville saw the bishop hit the ground. With growing anxiety he turned his horse.

At that same moment at Wotton House, William Evelyn, his brother and two friends were sitting in the dining room, when they thought they heard a noise outside. Turning to the window they were surprised to see Samuel Wilberforce looking in. William Evelyn recognised him immediately, having met the bishop on a number of occasions elsewhere. He was amazed that the bishop should pay a visit unannounced. After a while, when the butler did not enter to inform them they had a visitor, the party went outside but could find no sign of Wilberforce or his horse. A little later came the tragic news.

When Lord Granville dismounted by the side of the prostrate figure in Deerleap Wood there was nothing to be done. Soapy Sam was dead.

16

Take Me Home

MANY people experience at some moment in their lives an incident which cannot be explained by the normal criteria of life. Some quickly push such an occurrence to the back of their mind. 'I must have been dreaming or drinking', they say. Often there will be a reluctance to tell others of their experience lest they should be considered odd. Often, in the relaxed surroundings of home or hostelry, a mere hint or two will arouse our curiosity. When pressured some may tell us a little more, but often omit a time or place, leaving the ghost hunter with the flesh of a story but without its bones.

'But which house was it? Could it have been that street?'

'Ah! That I cannot say. Time slowed like in a dream and perhaps it was.'

Sometimes they will substitute a place or time, leaving the researcher unable to verify the story. A human tragedy, death or disaster, referred to but frustratingly missing when back copies of the local newspaper are searched. Dream, imagination, truth or a combination of the three, that judgement the writer leaves to the reader.

One dark, gloomy, wet Saturday night in 1947, a man was driving home in his van along the Portsmouth Road towards Cobham. The time was well after 11 o'clock. As he descended Tartar Hill he noticed a young girl at the side of the road, trying to wave him down. Now normally he would not have stopped in these circumstances but, without thinking, he found himself pulling to a halt outside the Tartar pub. The girl, who had been some way up the road, now appeared by the side of the van. He pushed open the door and silently she climbed in. She did not speak and he did not ask. The rain poured down, like the tapping of a thousand fingers upon the van roof. He waited but still nothing was said. She did not look at him but stared straight ahead, her pale skin reflecting the thin light coming from the pub. He would have waited longer.

He started the engine and slowly drove away down the hill, continuing his interrupted journey towards Cobham High Street. The girl still looked at the road glistening ahead, her dark, blank eyes impenetrable. A strange feeling, call it fear if you like, started in his stomach and seemed to spread slowly around his body, across his shoulders and up the back of his neck. The journey to the High Street took an age but fear gave way to irritation. Why would she not speak? He stopped in the High Street, thinking she might get out. She sat immobile, her hair strangely grey, her hands in her lap, no movement from her lips. But he could not speak to her.

He started up the van again and headed for home, hoping that at some point his silent companion would indicate somehow where she wanted to get out. He turned down Church Street just as the church clock was striking midnight. Suddenly the engine cut out and the vehicle coasted slowly to a stop by the side of the churchyard. Still saying nothing, the girl opened the door and got out. And still it rained. She took the man's coat, putting it over her head as she ran off. The man saw her flitting through the churchyard in the direction of a house on the far side.

He was tempted to go after her, but found he could not move. His arms felt like lead. How long he stayed like this he did not know, but eventually his hand moved to the ignition, the engine fired and the man drove slowly on his way.

He could not bring himself to mention this strange incident to either family or friends. About a week later, going about his normal business, he found himself driving once more down Church Street, Cobham. Curiosity got the better of him. He parked his van and threaded his way through the churchyard towards the house he presumed the girl had been making for. The door was opened by a smart, well-dressed man with a pleasant face, but the sharp lines round his mouth and eyes told of past tragedies.

'I have come to collect my coat. I think it was your daughter who borrowed it from me last week.'

The man smiled gently. 'So you've seen her too. You're not the first.' The man paused and continued. 'My daughter died in a fire in this house ten years ago. She had been out with friends, to the Tartar pub I believe. She came home later than she should have. It was the time we had the electricians here and that night we had no power, so she took a candle up to her bedroom. She must have been reading in bed and fallen asleep. Something must have knocked the candle over. It was the smoke that killed her.'

The driver mumbled something about how sorry he was.

'Let me take you to her grave. We had her buried just over there so she would still be near us.'

The van driver followed the father and once more found

himself threading his way through gravestones. They came to a well-kept grave, ablaze with flowers. The coat was lying on the gravestone. Just then a breeze got up, murmuring in the trees. The driver could hear the church clock striking, could see the wet road stretching before him. Something touched his arm and a quiet voice seemed to say: 'Thank you for taking me home.'

17

The Man with the Three Cornered Hat

'**W**HAT really is a ghost?' I asked my aunt, having heard the word on some radio programme she had just finished listening to.

'That's a difficult thing to answer, my boy,' she replied after a little thought. I remember wondering why most adults always replied to your question in that way. It was very annoying to an eight year old. I followed her into the kitchen.

'But please, I want to know!' I insisted. This was the early 1950s before many of us had television.

She smiled gently and turned away. She sat down at the tiny kitchen table, and looked up at the intricate patterns made by the cracks in the ceiling. She always looked up there when she was thinking. There was silence for a very long time. Then she took a deep breath, which at least told me that I was going to get some sort of an answer.

'It's when someone dies but for some reason decides to

come back to our world, or perhaps not to leave it,' she said quietly. 'Sometimes the ghost will look exactly like the person when they were alive,' she continued, anticipating my next question, hardly raising her voice above a whisper. 'Sometimes you will know they're there even though you can't see them.' She paused, resting her head on one arm, staring down at the lino. 'Lots of people don't believe in ghosts. They think that when you die, you're gone and that's it.'

'Do you believe in ghosts?' I asked with piping voice.

'Shush, laddie, or your uncle will hear.' Uncle had stayed in the backroom, sticking his stamps into a big red album. 'He always laughs and says ghosts are rubbish and can't be true but I . . .' and here she faltered.

'Yes, yes, please say,' I pleaded in a lowered voice.

She paused for even longer than before and once again looked up at the ceiling. 'Yes, I think I do. In fact, I know I do,' she ended emphatically.

I don't think she really wanted to hear my next question but it came out all the same. 'Have you ever seen a ghost?'

'Yes, I think I have. Not just one but several. They say that some people are better at seeing them than others.'

I waited impatiently through yet another long silence. She moved towards the sink to begin the washing up, showing no sign of telling more. 'Please tell me when you saw them, please!'

She looked me straight in the eye without a smile, her warm brown eyes as cold as I had ever seen them. I did not look away from her gaze but gave her my most serious expression in return. 'All right, I'll tell you about one occasion when I know I saw a ghost.' The smile which rarely left her face returned once more. 'But only if you help me with the wiping up!'

'It was before the war, even before your uncle and I were married, when we were courting. It was 1937, the year our late king was crowned. You know — his coronation, like Queen Elizabeth will have next year. We both lived at home in Merton then. Your uncle had just got a good job at the toy factory, so one of the first things he did afterwards was to go out and buy a car. Fortunately it was a bit bigger than the ones he helped to make! Not a new car, mind you, but very smart — a Morris Eight saloon. Lovely car it was. We had to give it up during the war. There was no petrol, you see.'

At this point I became a little worried that I would never hear about the ghost, only the usual war memories.

'Anyway, most Sundays in the summer we would go for drives out into the country, usually to somewhere like Box Hill. One of our favourite places that was, still is really, except we don't seem to go there any more. We'd drive up the Zigzag and stop the car above the southern slope. Sometimes I even managed to get your lazy uncle to go for a walk and we'd have a picnic. Other times your uncle stayed in the car, reading one of his books. Although he could be romantic at times, I can tell you!' she said emphatically.

'But I loved to walk. It's a curious place up there — full of atmosphere, of, how can I put it, presence, despite it often being crowded. The southern slope on one side of the road is all light and open with that glorious view across the Weald all the way to the South Downs. But the other side of the road to the north is a thicket of trees and bushes. The dark and the light in opposition across a tarmac divide. The good and evil, the living and the dead.'

She stopped a moment, gazing out of the kitchen window, letting a greasy plate slide back into the murky water.

'Well, one Sunday we set out from Merton in lovely sunny weather but by the time we were driving up the Zigzag, the air had become very heavy and blue-black clouds were rolling up from the Dorking direction. We stopped the car in our usual spot. But your uncle wouldn't come for a walk. It was going to rain and he had no intention of getting wet. The wind was getting up a bit and electricity was all around. Just the sort of weather I find exciting. Your uncle told me I was silly and he reminded me not to stand under any trees. Off I went, just as the first flashes of lightning rent the sky. I counted — then came the thunder, still some way away I worked out.'

This time there was another silence, as she minutely studied the intricate surface of a dirty plate.

'That Sunday I seemed drawn towards the dark side, which by now really was dark,' she continued softly. 'Without thinking about it, I found myself crunching through the carpet of leaf mould and twigs. Thunder rumbled again in the background. I walked further into the darkness of the thicket. Suddenly an almighty flash of lightning lit up the trees in a white glare and very, very quickly there came a tremendous crack of thunder. It seemed all around me.'

I looked in admiration at my aunt. I always knew that she was a very brave lady. My tea towel dropped to the floor.

'Pick it up, silly boy,' she scolded. 'Hmm, it's about time I cleaned that floor.'

I retrieved the tea towel from the dog's bowl. 'Go on, this is scary,' I said, not trying to hide my excitement.

'Well, I instinctively crouched down, not moving from the spot, when the thunder and lightning came. The wind howled through the trees above, bending their tops right over such was its force. There was the sound of cracking

101

branches above. I thought about running back to the car but something seemed to hold me to the spot and strangely it had not yet started raining. The wind grew even stronger, blowing through the thicket even at ground level and suddenly it was cold, almost icy cold. I began to shiver but straightened up when I saw a figure making its way through the undergrowth towards me. It was a man. He seemed almost to be driven by the wind. The first thing I noticed about him was that he was wearing an old-fashioned three cornered black hat, which was firmly fixed upon his head despite the gale now blowing with even greater ferocity. And he walked with a stick. As he came on ever nearer, I noticed other strange things about his clothes. He had a long coat on, blue I think it was, but it was difficult to tell in the strange light. It had bright buttons which seemed to flash in the lightning. His trousers were, well, breeches, I suppose you'd call them, and he had buckled shoes.'

'Did you think he was a ghost? Did you say anything to him?' I badgered.

'Yes, I was sure he wasn't alive like you and I. But no, I never thought of saying anything to him. It didn't seem necessary, but it wasn't because I was speechless with fright or anything like that. In fact, the sight of him made me feel calm, very calm, even in the midst of one of the worst thunderstorms your uncle can remember.'

She stared vacantly out of the kitchen window again. Then I saw her eyes switch back to the present. 'I think it's going to rain,' she mumbled. After what seemed an age, she continued her story.

'He came right up to me. That's when I noticed that he had only one eye. The other was almost closed, just a white slit showing. His clothes looked rather scruffy. He walked

102

on, leaning on his stick, but made no sign that he had seen me.
This was his world not mine. Perhaps I was a ghost in his. He
was talking very loudly, his voice easily rising above the almost
constant roar and crash of thunder. I caught a snatch of what
he said as he walked right past me. He seemed to be saying a
prayer: ". . . for Jesus Christ's sake, save us and the whole race
of mankind, as the returning prodigal." That's what he was
saying. I did not look round immediately when he had gone
by and suddenly came the rain, in soaking sheets even under
the trees. Eventually, when I did look round, of the man in
the three cornered hat there was no sign. Instead, there was
your uncle with an umbrella!'

Brownish green water gurgled down the plug hole; the
last cup for my attention was placed firmly upon the
wooden draining board.

'Who was he? Did you ever find out?'

'Your uncle, who had been getting a bit worried about
me, laughed himself silly, of course. But down in the
Burford Bridge, over a warming drink, I wondered if it
had anything to do with the man who was buried up on Box
Hill. You could see the stone which marked the spot where
he was buried, I expect you still can, but it's a long time
since I've been there. His name was Peter Labelliere and he
was buried there in 1800, according to the stone. The
fascinating thing was that he was buried head down.'

'What on earth for?'

'I didn't know and it was a long time before I found out
anything more about Mr Labelliere. The following year
your uncle and I were married and moved into this house,
brand new it was, we were very lucky. And then came the
war, but despite all the troubles then, with your uncle out in
India with the RAF, I never forgot what I had seen on Box
Hill that summer day.'

'I don't need to tell you that your uncle's always collected books,' she continued. 'Well, one day after the war, we were in a bookshop in the Charing Cross Road. It was nearly lunchtime, I remember, and I was starving, but your uncle wouldn't come away. I started looking along the packed shelves. Can't they put them in some sort of order, I thought. But then the title of one book caught my eye — *Recollections of Old Dorking* it was called. I began leafing through the pages and that's where I found the story of Peter Labelliere. He had been a major in the army who retired to lodgings in a small cottage in Dorking. He was eccentric to say the least. On his pension he could have afforded better, but he became a well-known local figure, particularly for his generosity to those less well-off than himself. But there were three things that seemed to confirm that he was the man I had seen those years before during the storm on Box Hill. Hold on, I'll go and get the book. I managed to persuade your uncle to buy it for me instead of lunch.'

She disappeared into the front room and came back clutching a book with a red cover. 'Now, where was it . . . ? Yes, here we are. Let me read you something.' We both sat down at the kitchen table.

'His dress, in which he was very negligent, was of that period — a long blue coat, with gilt buttons, knee breeches, worsted stockings, buckled shoes, and a three cornered black hat. That's him. I knew it was. Now, let's find the next bit . . . Major Labelliere was much given to meditation, and Box Hill was his favourite resort for this purpose, especially on the threatened approach of a thunderstorm. Then it says about him falling down in the undergrowth one day and gouging out his eye.'

She went on, reading further from the book. 'This sad

accident, it appears, happened at the favourite spot which he selected for his strange burial, and where it is said — I know not with what truth — that he once had a vision. It also says that he asked his landlady's children to dance on his coffin, perhaps to signify that his funeral should not be a sombre affair. There, I think that wraps it up, don't you?'

'But why was he buried head down?'

'There's something about that at the end here somewhere. Some say that it was because he thought the world so topsy-turvy in his day that, when it came right in the end, he would be the right way up! If that's true I think it must be disappointment that made him return, although strangely not on his head! I believe the second possibility. He was a very religious man and he wanted to be buried head down in imitation of St Peter, his namesake, who tradition says was crucified in that position.'

'The opposite way from Jesus?'

'Yes, that's right,' said my aunt, as she shut the book firmly, a sign to me that her story was finished.

'Does he still walk around Box Hill?'

'Ah, that I do not know. Perhaps when it seems like thunder we should go and see.'

18

Poltergeist at the Percy Arms

THERE are many tales of apparitions, poltergeist, strange sounds and other unexplained happenings in Surrey pubs. The county's hostelries have been the scene of so much human drama during the last four hundred years or so, that this is not surprising. The unconvinced may raise a wry smile and call it the 'spirit' of advertising. But not all the reported hauntings can be explained as a product of the brewery's advertising department or the landlord's desire for local newspaper coverage. Neither can they all be put down to customers' over indulgence!

The reports of strange occurrences in the Percy Arms, Chilworth, have spanned many years. Happenings, impossible to explain in any reasonably normal way, which have been experienced by many different people. Mrs Testar was landlady of the Percy Arms for more than twenty years, having taken over the pub in the 1950s. She soon discovered that the Percy Arms was the haunt of a restless spirit, a poltergeist.

Poltergeist literally means a ghost creating a disturbance and this is just what Mrs Testar, her staff and customers experienced. Doors would slam with great force and for no reason, while strange sounds like coal being shovelled were heard in the middle of the night. Objects would move from one side of a room to another but without human assistance. Even in the crowded bars tankards and stools would suddenly levitate and be thrown across the room. Mrs Testar's cousin was sceptical about the stories until, one night, he placed a glass of beer on the counter and it promptly sped off along the bar and smashed on the floor.

Head waiter, Bernard Wilson, reported an occasion when he was upstairs late one night after closing and heard a terrific rattle and crash sounding like someone violently shaking the shutters over the bar in the saloon. Thinking it might be burglars, he grabbed a poker, and rushed downstairs. All was undisturbed, the bar being empty, the shutters untouched.

In one particular bedroom where Mrs Testar slept the presence was very apparent at night. She felt a heavy pressure on her back and the weight of something lying on her bed. These unnerving happenings forced her to change rooms. Guests who subsequently stayed in the haunted bedroom often complained at breakfast of hearing strange noises in the night and feeling the weight of something sitting on their bed.

What was the secret of this restless spirit, who became so familiar to both staff and customers in the Percy Arms? Perhaps it returned because of something left undone before a violent end? Could history show any matter likely to be the cause? Did the straggling village of Chilworth and its nondescript looking pub have much history anyway?

Chilworth is an unusual village in many ways. Some

might call it ugly, in sharp contrast to the beautiful countryside surrounding it. Downland and tree-clad greensand hills topped by the ironstone church dedicated to St Martha look down on the valley of the little River Tillingbourne and a street of bland brick houses. Some of the houses have doors opening straight onto the pavement, reminiscent of the industrial towns of northern England. And here, of course, is a pointer to the place's history, for industry was at the heart of this remarkable village for several centuries.

Martin Tupper, the Victorian author and poet, who lived for much of his life in Albury, adjacent to Chilworth, waxed lyrically about the beauty of the Tillingbourne Valley. The river's clear, sparkling, trout-filled waters, flowed fast through pretty Shere, past Gomshall and Albury and on to Chilworth. Tupper lost no opportunity to put down his thoughts about the hills and woods of his homeland. One of his poems, written in the 1840s included these lines:

'Mammon, from those long white mills
With foggy steam the prospect fills;
Chimneys red with sulph'rous smoke
Blight those hanging groves of oak.'

Tupper was looking down on the infamous Chilworth Mills, just to the north of the village, where that tool of death and destruction, gunpowder, had been manufactured since 1625. A Dante's inferno, a hell on earth if ever there was one, where the merest spark could blow the millworkers beyond this earth. And often it did.

Ownership of the mills passed through many hands down the years but in the 19th century they became the property of the Duke of Northumberland. The family name of the Duke was Percy, hence the name of the local inn. To the inn came coroner and jury to investigate the latest tragedy at the mills. Often, it is said, the few poor fragments of the victims came too, shattered beyond all hope of recognition.

The first three gunpowder mills established at Chilworth blew up within a few short months of being built. The same story continued through the centuries. By the second half of the 19th century safety precautions were stringent. Workers wore special clothing and in the danger areas special shoes, for the smallest spark from a metal button or boot stud could spell oblivion. But still the sound of tragedy erupted with regularity, echoing loud and long from valley to hill and back again, striking fear in the hearts of the wives and children of Chilworth who heard it.

Fatal explosions occurred in 1864, 1874, 1879 and 1883 for example. But the tragedy most easily recalled from the corporate memory of the village was the 'Great Explosion' of 1901, in which six men lost their lives. Could the poltergeist at the Percy Arms be the spirit of one of those men, whose life was cut short in such a violent instant?

It was twenty minutes to nine on the frosty morning of Tuesday 12th February when the chill air above Chilworth village was rent by a fearsome explosion. Smoke shot high into the sky and rubble was hurled in all directions — bricks, sheets of corrugated iron, baulks of timber, bits of machinery and twisted pieces of human remains.

When rescuers reached the scene there was little left to rescue. Three men, Walter Abbot, William Prior and William Marshall had been loading a tramway trolley outside a building known as the Black Corning House. Inside the house, where the gunpowder in cake form was crushed and granulated into powder, George Smithers, William Sopp and Robert Chandler had been about to restart the machinery following their short stop for breakfast. Now there was nothing left but a heap of wreckage. The trees around the building were blasted, blackened or uprooted, their remaining branches festooned with shattered timbers, charred and burning clothing and strands of human flesh.

The three men working the trolley had been blown apart. Portions of one of them were found in a meadow 150 yards away. The mangled trunk of another lay by the side of a blast protection wall, while the third victim was discovered in various places. His body had fallen on the tramway, one leg was elsewhere and one arm was a quarter of a mile away.

Of the men in the Corning House, Sopp was found dying in the rubble; Chandler, who was only 19, was everywhere, while Smithers had been thrown a hundred yards into a meadow. Incredibly, searchers discovered him still alive. Aged 45, he was the oldest of the men and had worked at the mills for 34 years. Although horribly injured poor George Smithers lived on until eleven o'clock that morning before released from his agony. Before the end he kept trying to say something, but all that came out was 'my arm! my arm!', so terribly smashed was that limb. Was he trying to tell them how and why it happened?

To the Percy Arms came coroner and jury to study the horrific facts as the still living saw them, and to visit the scant remains of the dead lying in the mill hospital. No one was to blame but the mill owners would make improvements, they concluded. Accidental death they all agreed.

The man who suffered most from the horrendous

results of one small spark was George Smithers. It may be that for vengeance's sake this unfortunate man could find no peace. Seeking a release, he vent his anger and frustration for such a violent and agonising death by haunting the Percy Arms. It is probably just coincidence but when the staff and customers there sought a nickname for their ghostly visitor, they called him George.

19

A Tsar in Surrey

THIS is my own ghost story. A minor occurrence, yes, but one which cannot be dismissed by any normal explanation. They say that some people are more susceptible than others to psychic phenomena, but I am not one of those people. However, I am sure that one evening in a Godalming pub something or someone from the past, for a very brief moment, succeeded in bypassing my lack of sensitivity in these matters. Even the slightest hint of the supernatural can radically alter your attitudes and remove your scepticism. It certainly did for me.

'Did you see that?' asked Tom, as I returned from the bar with a packet of crisps.

'Yes, I see you've managed to spill beer all over the carpet,' I replied sarcastically. Tom looked perplexed indeed. He certainly wasn't drunk, because he never had more than two halves in an evening. 'How did you do that?' I continued.

'But I didn't. One minute my glass was there, right there in the middle of the table, and then it suddenly lifted up and fell upon the floor,' he insisted.

'I believe you,' I replied without a hint of sincerity. Tom was quiet for a while. Then our conversation started up again, and we continued our discussion about an archaeological dig in the town, in which we were involved.

When I had half finished the crisps, I put the packet down on the table in front of me, and then a very odd thing happened. Without warning and without there being even the hint of a breeze from an open door, the packet suddenly sped off across the table and decanted its contents upon the floor. Was what I saw true, I asked myself? Am I dreaming or is this all imagination? As I turned to bend down to pick up the mess, my glass fell over and the best part of two-thirds of a pint of Burton ale flooded off the table and cascaded upon the floor.

'See, now you've done it too!' exclaimed Tom, breaking into my thoughts.

'It must have been a rush of air from outside when someone came in,' I suggested. 'And perhaps I caught my glass with my elbow,' I concluded. But did I? My elbow had been nowhere near that glass of beer. What had really moved that crisp packet in the motionless air? What, indeed! This place is supposedly haunted. Should I now begin to believe in ghosts?

Tom Maile and I were sitting in the bar of one of the most prominent buildings in Godalming's narrow High Street — the King's Arms Royal Hotel. Its magnificent facade is dated 1753 and built in chequered brick. It looks, perhaps, a little more in keeping with a town on the Bath Road in Berkshire than a Surrey town where a variety of industries once prospered.

The sign above its pillared entrance shows the arms of Henry VIII, suggesting an inn of ancient origins. Inside, exposed timbers and fine panelling confirm the presence of a building considerably older than the frontage. Over the centuries the inn has had many royal visitors including King Frederick William III of Prussia and Prince Leopold, later to become Leopold I, King of the Belgians, and Tsar Alexander of Russia.

On a dark winter's night, with a log fire burning in the bar and a glass of ale in the hand, figures from the past seem to haunt every nook and cranny of this venerable pile, glimpsed by some from the far corner of the eye and gone. As various parts of the building react to temperature changes, the creaks and groans seem as audible as your companion's chatter.

Strange happenings have been reported here on many occasions by both staff and visitors. Others have experienced inexplicable mishaps just as Tom Maile and I did that evening. Glasses and various other objects have been hurled across a room unaided by the hand of any living person. But sometimes, I am told, there comes the sound of heavy boots, the crash of breaking glass, the raucous laughter and the unintelligible banter of a foreign tongue. The sound of revelry above, coming from an empty room — for this is a party without guests and the source of all the noise is thin air.

Who or what is the cause of such a haunting? Perhaps an answer lies somewhere in the history of the place.

The town of Godalming grew prosperous in the Middle Ages thanks to the popularity of its woollen cloth, but this industry declined in the early 17th century. The town then switched to the production of knitted stockings in wool, silk and cotton. Later a great variety of knitted garments were produced and the industry still continues in the town to this day. Tanning, leather and skin working, papermaking and stone quarrying have also employed many generations of Godhelmians.

Portsmouth was an important naval centre from the time of Henry VIII and, following the restoration of Charles II in 1660, its facilities grew rapidly. Consequently the traffic on the road between the nation's capital and its premier naval port also greatly increased. The journey by cart or carriage was long and many inns were established along the route to give weary travellers refreshment and lodging.

In Surrey, towns and villages like Kingston, Esher, Ripley, Cobham, Guildford and Godalming all had their famous hostelries. The inns of Guildford were justly famous, but many an exhausted traveller preferred to push on those extra four miles to sample the delights offered in Godalming. There were many establishments to choose from — The White Hart, The Red Lion, The George, but most important of the town's coaching inns was the King's Arms. In the heyday of the Portsmouth Turnpike the London coach, 'Accommodation', stopped here.

In the reign of Charles II, Samuel Pepys often passed this way in his capacity as Secretary to the Admiralty. In the 18th and early 19th centuries the list of the famous was endless. One story, which has been passed down through the years, told of two English Dukes who stopped at the King's Arms to eat a mutton chop and take a glass of claret. So good was the fare provided that, when they finally left they had consumed eighteen chops each and drunk five bottles of claret!

The inn was run for many years by successive generations of the Moon family and, in 1698, it was James Moon who found himself providing sustenance and lodging for none other than Tsar Peter the Great, who was returning from Portsmouth with his entourage of twenty-one Russian noblemen and followers. Peter was ruthless in his determination to modernise his medieval nation. He toured western Europe, sometimes in disguise, to see how things were done. He went to Holland and then came to England. The diarist and horticulturist, John Evelyn, whose country seat was Wotton House near Dorking, was persuaded by King William to give up his London home, Sayes Court, Deptford, for three months for the benefit of the Russian party.

Peter was particularly interested in establishing a Russian navy along the lines of those of the most important sea-faring nations. He visited shipyards and then went to Portsmouth to watch two sham battles by ships of the English Navy. When they arrived in Godalming the Russian party was in boisterous mood. Soon the wine and brandy began to flow, while the pretty girls of Godalming ran for cover. They were also hungry, their appetites seemingly inexhaustable, as they proceeded to consume a prodigious quantity of food.

Some at least of this vast mound of food failed to reach the stomachs of the drunken revellers. Instead, they threw great chunks of meat across the room at each other along with many of the landlord's most expensive glasses. When the party finally ended, Peter the Great departed for John Evelyn's house in Deptford, much to the relief of the whole of Godalming. The Russians left behind a devastated inn, many shocked and frightened Godhelmians and a very large unpaid account! Apparently it was finally settled from the English royal purse.

At Deptford, where they stayed three months, the visitors' conduct seems hardly to have improved. They caused £150 worth of damage to Evelyn's house and garden. It was the state of his garden which most upset the diarist, for the Russians had ploughed through ornamental hedges during a number of drunken wheel-barrow races. Evelyn recorded in his diary that his bailiff had described them succinctly as 'right nasty'.

Peter and his countrymen finally returned to their homeland, where the young Tsar laid the foundations of modern Russia and, in so doing, earned the epithet 'great'. From his point of view, the trip to England had been a significant success. Perhaps he and his men remembered the 'happy' night they had spent in Godalming and carried the memory to the grave and beyond. Did one of the Russian noblemen sweep my crisps off the table that evening, or decant two-thirds of a pint of good English ale upon the floor? Maybe I was honoured with the presence of Tsar Peter himself — I would certainly like to think so!

20

Vengeance at Pitt Place

LORD Lyttleton awoke from a clammy, unrestful sleep, his senses jarred, beads of perspiration running down his forehead. A strange noise had brought him from those unplumbed depths of the nightmare world. The noise came on again, seemingly from above his head. It was the fluttering of a bird, there could be no mistake. For a moment he kept his eyes tightly closed, hoping that the sound would go away. But it was not to be. He jerked his eyes open and stared out into the suffocating blankness of his airless bedroom. The noise continued. Gradually before his fear-filled eyes there appeared a white bird, hovering. Slowly, as the bird rose and fell to the beating of its wings, to the nobleman's horror it turned into a woman. She was dressed in white, revenge written in every line of her haggard face. It was a woman he recognised, a woman whom he knew had good cause to hate him. It was a woman he knew was dead.

Mrs Amphlett was her name. Two of her daughters were asleep somewhere in his house at that very moment and she was standing, a menacing spectre, at the foot of the bed.

Her lips began to move. 'Prepare to die,' they echoed slowly. 'You will not exist three days,' and with that, she was gone. In panic, the nobleman gasped and struggled for air, screaming loudly for his manservant. The servant found his master in a great state of agitation. It was another of his master's attacks, just like those he had suffered in Ireland shortly before returning to his London house at Hill Street, Berkeley Square.

Next morning found Lord Lyttleton morose and thoughtful. He tried to impress upon his house guests the seriousness of his 'vision' the night before, but they were inclined to take it lightly. Throughout the morning he showed many signs of being greatly troubled by the event and perhaps he had good cause to be.

Lord Lyttleton was thirty-five and had succeeded to his title six years earlier, in 1773. His father had left him substantial property in Ireland and England, including Pitt Place, a fine house situated in Epsom. Although married, Lord Lyttleton had deserted his wife, Apphia, preferring the company of ladies somewhat younger than himself. Some described him as eccentric, others considered him to be a rake who led an immoral life of dissipation and indolence. In part this was true, but he had also begun to make a name for himself in politics and had spoken eloquently on several occasions in the House of Lords. Despite his private life, a successful political career seemed in prospect.

It was in Worcestershire that Lord Lyttleton met Mrs Amphlett, or, more importantly to him, her three young daughters. He was immediately smitten by the trio, aged fifteen, seventeen and nineteen. Their names were Christianna, Elizabeth and Margaret. He set out upon a path of seduction and in this he seems to have succeeded. By the early days of the following year the girls had been lured away from their pious mother, who soon languished and died. She passed away broken-hearted, revenge upon her lips, deep hate for the man who had done this driving her spirit to return. And thus she appeared before Lord Lyttleton in the early hours of 25th November 1779.

By the afternoon of that day, Lord Lyttleton's guests — Hugh, later Lord Fortescue, Lady Flood and the two Amphlett girls — had persuaded him that it was, indeed, merely a dream. Reinvigorated, Lord Lyttleton made his way to the House of Lords, where he showed his mettle by making an impressive speech about Ireland. Throughout that evening and the next day he appeared to be in good humour, enjoying life to the full as he always did.

On the morning of the third day, Saturday 27th November, Lord Lyttleton breakfasted with his friends. He was in cheerful mood, saying 'I have jockied the ghost, as this is the third day'. The party, now joined by Captain (later Admiral) Wolseley, drove down to Epsom in Lord Lyttleton's carriage to stay a few days at Pitt Place. As the carriage passed a graveyard on route, Lord Lyttleton remarked to Hugh Fortescue on the number of 'vulgar fellows' who died at the age of thirty-five. 'But you and I, who are gentlemen, shall live to a good old age,' he said emphatically, keeping his thoughts to himself.

Pitt Place was a fine Georgian house, probably the most impressive in the whole of Epsom. It had started life as a small farmhouse built in the middle of a large chalk pit. In fact, this was the origin of the name and in Lyttleton's time the name was spelled without the final 't'. The building had been added to piecemeal by a succession of owners but it was Lord Lyttleton's father, the first Baron, who had turned it into a fine mansion. The older parts of the building had low ceilings and great thick walls, while later parts were lofty and majestic. Some of the carved stonework was said to have come from Henry VIII's palace of Nonsuch. The house was rich in interior woodwork and much of the panelling was wonderfully carved. In Lord Lyttleton's bedroom, grotesque masks stared out from the wood surrounds of windows and doors.

That afternoon the party arrived at the house in plenty of time to prepare for dinner. Lyttleton seemed fit and cheerful and very little was said of the nightmare vision of nearly three days ago. It was best pushed to the back of the mind, lest it crawled into the merriment of the evening's entertainment. The host mentioned it only in jest claiming to have 'bilked the ghost'. But he went to bed earlier than expected, anxious perhaps to get the last night over and greet another day. Anxious for a future which revenge from beyond the grave could, surely, not deny him?

One of Lord Lyttleton's closest friends was Miles Andrews, whose country house was at Dartford in Kent. On the night of 27th November Andrews gave a large party at his home and, among his guests, he was expecting Lyttleton. But his friend, disturbed by his dream of Mrs Amphlett, had decided to go to Epsom for the weekend, rather than journey to Dartford, a decision which had not reached Andrews. The party at Dartford did not go well for Miles Andrews. He began to feel feverish as the evening wore on and suspected a chill brought on by the damp of late autumn travel. He went up to bed shortly before eleven o'clock, leaving his guests to their own devices.

Andrews slept in a four poster bed. He drew the curtains

around the bed to shut out the party's clamour and ease his aching head. But, before he had time to reach even the broken sleep of fever, the curtains at the foot of the bed were suddenly flung back. In the gloom Andrews could see his missing friend. Lyttleton was wearing a nightgown which was always kept in the Dartford house exclusively for his use. His friend had arrived at last, if somewhat late, but he had promised positively that he would come. Andrews thought that Lyttleton was about to play one of his usual practical jokes, something that he was in no mood for.

'You are at some of your tricks. Go to bed or I will throw something at you!' he cried.

Lyttleton frowned and replied, 'It's all over with me, Andrews. It's all over.'

Andrews considered this to be part of the joke. He grabbed hold of the nearest thing he could, a slipper, and hurled it at the outline of his friend. Lyttleton retreated to the adjacent dressing room, a room which had no separate exit. Andrews then jumped out of bed and rushed into the dressing room. He felt annoyed that Lyttleton had so startled him. But his friend was not there. He had certainly not passed back into the bedroom but had vanished somehow. His nightgown was found, undisturbed, in its usual place. Perplexed and angry Andrews went back to bed. Clever though his friend's disappearing act had been, he could not forgive him.

'Tell Lyttleton that there is no bed for him here. He'll have to find one at the inn for playing such a trick on a sick man,' he told his servant. But Lyttleton was nowhere to be found.

Next morning, one of Miles Andrews' guests, Mrs Pigou, left early for London and found the capital already buzzing with the news.

At Pitt Place Lord Lyttleton had gone to bed at about eleven o'clock the night before. His servant had mixed him his usual bedtime drink of rhubarb and mint water but, lacking a spoon near at hand, had stirred the concoction with an old tooth pick. His master had called him a 'slovenly dog' for doing so and ordered him to fetch the spoon. When the servant returned he found Lord Lyttleton lying on his back in bed, his chin pushed into his chest by the mound of pillows behind his head. Lyttleton was in the midst of a fit, gasping for breath and life itself. In panic, the servant ran for help, leaving his master to a lonely, choking death, his hand held out, trying to reach towards, perhaps, the smiling face of Mrs Amphlett. He died at exactly the time that he appeared at the foot of Miles Andrews' bed in Dartford, over twenty miles away.

When Andrews heard the tragic news he remembered the figure of his friend at the end of his bed that sad night. He also remembered how he had treated him in his time of need. Andrews broke down and it was to be a full three years before he recovered.

James Boswell recorded the opinion of Dr Johnson on the matter when he raised it in conversation a few years after the event. Johnson was taking tea at the house of Dr Adams.

'It is the most extraordinary thing that has happened in my day,' said Johnson. 'I heard it with my own ears from his uncle, Lord Westcote. I am so glad to have every evidence of the spiritual world, that I am almost willing to believe it,' he continued.

'You have evidence enough: good evidence, which needs no such support,' said Dr Adams.

'I like to have more,' replied the wise Dr Johnson.

Meanwhile, the unfortunate Lord Lyttleton slept

peacefully in his grave, never to return to Dartford or Epsom. The scene of his strange demise, Pitt Place, was demolished in 1967 and any secrets his panelled bedroom held went with the rubble.

The circumstances of the nobleman's death have passed into modern folklore, to be repeated and embellished as the years went by. This account has been based on early sources and tells the story as near to the truth as is now possible. But few could disagree with Johnson's final thoughts on the strange death of Lord Lyttleton.

Index